PROFESSIONAL LIABILITY and RISK MANAGEMENT

Bruce E. Bennett
Brenda K. Bryant
Gary R. VandenBos
Addison Greenwood

American Psychological Association
Washington, D.C. 20036

Published by
American Psychological Association
1200 Seventeenth Street, NW
Washington, DC 20036

Copies may be ordered from
APA Order Department
P.O. Box 2710
Hyattsville, MD 20784

Cover designed by Debra E. Riffe
Typeset by Harper Graphics, Waldorf, MD
Printed by Lancaster Press, Lancaster, PA
Technical editing and production coordinated by Valerie Montenegro

Library of Congress Cataloging-in-Publication Data

Professional liability and risk management/Bruce E. Bennett . . . [et al.].
   p.   cm.
  Includes bibliographical references.
  ISBN 1-55798-101-9
  1. Psychologists—Professional ethics—United States.
2. Psychologists—Complaints against—United States.
3. Psychologists—Malpractice—United States.   4. Insurance,
Malpractice—United States.   5. Risk management—United States.
I. Bennett, Bruce E.
BF76.4.P77   1990
174'.915—dc20

90-1199
CIP

Printed in the United States of America.
First edition

Contents

Foreword

Over the past decade psychologists have witnessed a lack of availability of professional liability insurance as well as steady increases in malpractice insurance premiums. Recent increases in insurance rates strongly suggest that more than inflation is contributing to the premiums paid by the more than 33,000 psychologists covered under the Professional Liability Program designed by the American Psychological Association Insurance Trust (APAIT) for members of the American Psychological Association (APA).

A lack of information regarding the linkage of professional practice, ethics, professional liability, and insurance has undoubtedly contributed to the increase in premiums. This information void is being filled by the publication of *Professional Liability and Risk Management*, which is being distributed, free of charge, to all psychologists currently insured under the APAIT-endorsed Professional Liability Program.

This project, funded by the APAIT, is one of a series of risk management activities designed to help psychologists deal with difficult situations, to reduce the likelihood of litigation, and to initiate "damage control" measures should a malpractice suit be filed. It is hoped that this monograph will promote greater awareness of areas of potential liability and risk management techniques associated with such liability.

Professional Liability and Risk Management is required reading for all psychologists. Read it to familiarize yourself with the critical areas of practice, ethics, insurance, and malpractice. Use it as a starting point for additional research into areas of interest. Keep it on your desk as a ready reference resource.

This volume is not intended to dictate standards of care. It will not tell you how to practice psychology in a risk-free environment. It will not prevent a malpractice suit. It can, however, give you reference points to enhance professional and ethical practice. And it can limit your exposure to a potential suit and increase your effectiveness in handling a threatened or actual suit.

Although there is no fail-safe mechanism to avoid a malpractice suit, awareness of key practice, ethics, and malpractice issues is essential in risk management. Remember that awareness can limit the expenses associated with litigation and can minimize the stresses associated with a malpractice suit.

The American Psychological Association Insurance Trust is to be commended for providing the funding and expertise that brought this monograph into existence. The APAIT is more than the organization that reviews and endorses our member malpractice program. It is committed to reducing professional liability risk exposures for psychologists as individuals and for the profession as a whole.

Faith Tanney
Chair, APA Committee for the Advancement
of Professional Practice

Acknowledgments

This volume is the result of an active collaboration between the American Psychological Association Insurance Trust (APAIT) and the American Psychological Association (APA). The development of *Professional Liability and Risk Management* was supported by a grant from the American Psychological Association Insurance Trust.

Beginning in the early 1980s, it became apparent in discussions between the APAIT and the APA that a brief primer on ethics, practice guidelines, and professional liability was needed. Various draft tables of contents were developed in the mid-1980s. By 1987, the basic plan for this volume was established. Those trustees who were particularly noteworthy in the final collaboration and development of the volume include Mary Henle; John J. McCormack, Jr.; John R. Murray III; Paul L. O'Brien; A. Eugene Shapiro; Joan G. Willens; and Charles D. Speilberger (then APA Treasurer and current APA President-elect). Other trustees who have helped bring this book to fruition include Judith E. N. Albino; Bruce L. Boyd; Patricia M. Bricklin; Raymond D. Fowler; Bruce Sales; and Leon VandeCreek.

The authors of this volume wish to extend a special thanks to Margaret A. Bogie, Executive Administrator of the APAIT, for her active participation throughout the development and production of this project and for her technical expertise on professional liability insurance.

We also acknowledge those who provided substantive feedback on various outlines and drafts of this volume throughout its development, including David H. Mills and Faith Tanney; and we owe special thanks to Donald N. Bersoff for providing commentary from a legal perspective.

Finally, we extend our gratitude to the numerous staff members at the APA who have been involved in the development and production of this volume, especially to Rick Sample, APA Librarian; to Donna Stewart, Julia Frank-McNeil, Mary Lynn Skutley, and Valerie Montenegro for their insightful suggestions and expert editing; and to Patricia Harding-Clark and Janet E. Cole for proofreading and administrative assistance.

A Note to Nonclinicians and Those Who Provide Services Other Than Mental Health Care

At first glance, one might view this monograph as a risk management primer aimed solely at psychologists engaged in the delivery of health care services. Indeed, much of the content is oriented in that direction. As such, *Professional Liability and Risk Management* is a must for psychologists practicing in the health care arena.

Upon closer examination, however, it will become apparent that the risk management techniques and procedures discussed herein extend well beyond direct clinical practice. The sections dealing with evaluation and testing have direct applicability to industrial/organizational and school psychologists or those who use psychological procedures for the selection, retention, or promotion of employees in the business or corporate setting.

Finally, research and academic psychologists will find many examples designed to raise awareness of potential areas of litigation in their occupational spheres and methods of managing those specific risks.

The Professional Liability Malpractice Policy endorsed by the APAIT provides coverage for the entire spectrum of psychological services. The issues addressed in this monograph, therefore, touch on the activities and practices of all psychologists.

Introduction

Practitioners in the many branches of psychology have two activities in common: They continuously exercise professional judgment in matters related to the sometimes problematic actions of other human beings, and, in the best interest of those human beings, they accept the responsibility for delivering a cornucopia of decisions and recommendations that affect the lives of their clients, clients' families, and those with whom clients work. In order to do these things effectively, the practitioner must learn to listen, analyze, and speak with exceptional skill and to do so in a social context that can be fraught with conflict, misunderstanding, and error. Decisions must be made in relation to several distinct considerations:

- The practitioner's primary humanitarian mission—to bring all of his or her training, skill, judgment, and commitment to the treatment of the client;
- The practitioner's personal ethics and the ethical principles for psychologists that he or she is obliged by legal and professional codes to maintain;
- The practitioner's professional and legal liability for the nature and quality of care delivery, which represents the practitioner's point of exposure to civil lawsuits and to the requirements of laws regulating conduct as a licensed professional; and
- The practitioner's level of basic business skill in providing service and maintaining the best standards of delivery so that neither the practitioner, nor the clients, nor the practice itself will suffer.

The relation between these components of professional life—mission, ethics and responsibility, liability, and business—is complex. In some instances, one component takes precedence over all others. At other times, each component appears to have equal weight. When there is conflict, the conflict can most often be resolved with little difficulty. However, there are times when one component overpowers one or more of the others, and the resolution of conflict is not easy, nor are the results satisfactory in all ways. Inseparable from all decisions the practitioner makes, however, is his or her duty to the client, the primary ethical principle guiding the conduct of the practitioner's professional life.

The reality of practicing as a psychologist is that this balancing act is not always successful. There are times when a client or a client's family is not satisfied with the results of the services offered. The client may have unrealistic expectations about what should happen while he or she is receiving services. The practitioner's actions indeed may be inappropriate or unethical. In such instances, the client or someone representing the client's interests may question the practitioner's ability to deliver appropriate services. Usually such questions can be resolved by discussion, or, if the client is not satisfied with the answers, he or she can be referred to another therapist. At other times, no agreement can be reached, and the client may bring a lawsuit for malpractice against the psychologist—an action well within the rights of clients.

Some suits are neither justified nor justifiable. The client's emotional and psychological disturbance may cause him or her to misinterpret what has occurred, or the client simply may not understand the process of therapy and its goals. Instituting a suit may be the client's way of striking out at the psychologist. And, regrettably, there are also times that the client's goal may be nothing more than personal gain. In many cases, too, the client's claims are not frivolous.

It is too often the case that when a psychologist is faced with the threat or the reality of a lawsuit, he or she is at a loss about how to proceed. In school, practitioners develop a basic foundation in substantive and clinical matters. Thereafter, they rely on experience, discussions with colleagues, current surveys of literature, and the occasional seminar to refine and refresh their expertise. However, in matters of the law, malpractice, and the relation of professional liability insurance to everyday work, many practitioners never acquire a foundation, or if they do, they do so in an ad hoc manner—through personal reading, continuing education activities, or in reaction to rumors and "horror stories" that routinely echo around highly publicized cases. The study of the laws that govern psychology and the concept of malpractice in relation to those laws is not yet a fundamental part of most training programs, even those leading to a doctoral degree in clinical psychology. Moreover, the majority of practitioners find that if they have an interest, they have little time to both learn the law and practice their profession.

Thus, in spite of the importance of understanding the laws that govern their practice and the tools they need to protect themselves, most practitioners act on the faith that their training will protect them. When they purchase professional liability insurance (PLI), they do so with little understanding of its purpose and limitations. In general, because they consider themselves skilled and ethical, they find the terms of PLI, the concept of malpractice, and the actions of the courts in interpreting the laws that govern malpractice to be academic or arcane knowledge of little use to *them*. At the same time, they continue to harbor an undercurrent of concern and acknowledge that they are poorly versed on malpractice and on what their insurance does and does not cover. Lacking this knowledge, psychologists are unable to develop a solid strategy for accommodating these fundamental considerations in the conduct of their clinical practice.

What This Book Does and Does Not Do

This volume is not a technical exposition written by lawyers and insurance representatives. Rather, it is a volume prepared by practitioners for practitioners who are faced with the complexities of everyday decision making. It does not provide all the answers one would need if one were sued, or even answers that will always be correct. Laws and circumstances can change, and opinions differ about how practitioners should conduct themselves or about what specific things they should, or should not do. In preparing this volume, we followed one guiding principle: the contents are confined to what practitioners need to know or should consider. There are three goals: (a) to provide a practical manual that demonstrates how the ethical principles within which a practitioner must operate can be applied in a real world; (b) to help practitioners understand how the laws governing practice work; and (c) to explain some of the basics of how the system that protects practitioners, including insurance, can work for practitioners.

This book was designed to answer the questions about professional liability that are asked by all mental health practitioners, not just psychologists. To answer those questions, we have drawn from information found in numerous books and articles about malpractice and liability insurance as well as from related material sponsored and written by the American Psychological Association Insurance Trust (APAIT). The APAIT data, to the best of our knowledge, is the single best collection of statistical information available on the subject of psychological malpractice. Thus it offers an unusually direct view into the subject of malpractice as it relates to psychologist–practitioners in America. Also, because explanations of terms and the mechanics of their applications were readily available from the APAIT, we have used APAIT-sponsored insurance policies as a basis for discussing professional liability insurance and its workings. Some carriers may use different terminology or have different procedures.

We believe that the principles and information discussed in this volume provide a thorough and accurate picture of professional liability and its relation to the practitioner and may be generally applicable to all practitioners. However, it is not our intent to provide legal advice in relation to malpractice suits. The realities of such suits may have quite different concerns and implications. This book is intended to explain why practitioners should have protection against possible suits, not to sell insurance in general or the policies sponsored by the APAIT in particular. Carriers that provide PLI do so directly to practitioners. (By law, casualty insurance cannot be sold on a group basis.) The particular professional liability insurance policy made available through the APAIT to qualified members of the American Psychological Association (APA) is specially crafted to take into account the standards and practices to which APA members are sworn. The carrier that insures APA members through the APAIT-sponsored program also offers different policies to many types of practitioners who are not members of the APA. Other insurance companies, to a lesser degree, also offer coverage.

What To Look For

This volume has five chapters, which fall into two sections. Part I (chapters 1 to 3) focuses on the practical meanings of malpractice, duty of care, ethics, the law, and liability insurance and how they interact. Chapter 1 provides a few examples of the types of suits brought against psychologists from all specialties. Chapter 2 discusses the real meaning of ethics and practice guidelines. Chapter 3 discusses the nature of professional liability and its relation to practice. Part II (chapters 4 and 5) provides suggestions about how practitioners can integrate safeguards into daily practice that will best accommodate the interests of clients and practitioners. These practical suggestions appear in chapter 4 in the form of focus lists. Next, chapter 5 explains the role and structure of professional liability insurance. We have used the word *client* (rather than *patient* or *client and patient*) because this volume is directed not only to psychotherapists but also to industrial and organizational consultants, school counselors, and other practitioners, and to academics—indeed, to all psychologists who provide services that require them to apply the *Ethical Principles of Psychologists* (APA, 1990) and the practice guidelines of the profession, and to do so within the context of the law. Many of the principles in this volume apply equally well to other practitioners providing mental health services.

In Closing

No one volume or even a collection of volumes, however exhaustive, can provide the ultimate answers to questions about liability or practice within the context of liability. This book does not discuss what one *should* do. Our mission in this volume is to provide factual information and suggestions, an overview of what could happen under certain circumstances, and some responses that might be useful for confronting those events should they arise.

The one instance in this discussion that you will be told what you should do is right here: Keep practicing. If you do not already know how to do so, learn to recognize the limitations *and* the liberties imposed by the laws that govern practice. Learn how to safeguard both yourself and your clients from the sometimes inadequate or confusing rules and regulations imposed upon you as a professional. Continue to apply the skills that you have learned, guided by the highest principles that govern the conduct of all responsible professionals.

Part I

Ethics, Practice Guidelines, and Liability

1

Professional Ethics and Practice Guidelines: How They Affect You

Do these phrases sound familiar to you?

- How could she (or he) have been that stupid? Didn't she (or he) realize that the client would file a complaint?
- I just don't know what to tell you. Your client must have misunderstood what you were trying to do, but that doesn't help you. The complaint has been filed. You have to deal with it.

In hindsight, the proper decision or path is often stunningly clear. However, it is important for us to nurture the objectivity that will strengthen our foresight and allow us to make the correct decision before the fact.

This volume examines the ethics and practice guidelines that apply to our work and identifies those instances when we are vulnerable to behaving unprofessionally, inappropriately, unthinkingly, ignorantly, and even in a way that does harm to our clients. Most important, it describes learning to practice in a way that upholds the ethics and practice guidelines that we ourselves have established for our profession.

The ethics and practice guidelines that we were taught in school and in the early days of our career often lose definition as we grow older. The pressures of everyday life lead us to view them as abstract concepts that we believe are ingrained in us. We do not often stop and consciously consider what they mean in relation to the realities of practicing today. Perhaps the only time we think about ethics is when we hear about the trouble a colleague is having. Some practitioners view ethics either as rules designed to hinder our innocent colleagues and selves or to use as a lever to remove colleagues who may not be as concerned about themselves, their clients, or the profession as we might be. We go along, year after year, providing services without consciously reviewing how we provide those services.

Too often, we fail to evaluate our own performance, attitudes, behaviors, and work skills objectively in terms of the ethics and practice guidelines of the profession. We operate on automatic control, thinking that we are working on the part of our professions that really counts—helping the client. After all, we are protected by our professional armor. But the armor we wear limits our view.

The case examples that follow, which are based on actual liability cases, demonstrate that even the best intentions, even the most innocent of practices, can lead to complications for ourselves and our colleagues. They also show that a little forethought can affect the outcome of almost any situation.

Example 1: A Clinician Does a Good Deed

Dr. D was pleased to see increasing signs of independence and a growing ability to take control on the part of the client, who had been in treatment for some time. When the client came to Dr. D with a plan for going into business with a friend, Dr. D even spent some time discussing the perils and perks of being one's own boss. A few months into the business, the new bosses ran into financial trouble. Dr. D's client came to Dr. D very depressed and expressed fears of "failing again," saying, "If we just had another $15,000 to tide us over until the end of the quarter, when all our order payments come due, just $15,000." Dr. D thought quickly and volunteered to provide the additional financing, as a loan secured by a part of the assets of the business. Eventually, an agreement was made between Dr. D, the client, and the client's partner.

Dr. D continued to treat the client. After a few months had passed and the time for repaying the loan had come and gone, Dr. D began to ask the client for the repayment. Eventually, Dr. D had to contact a lawyer and sue the client and the client's partner for repayment. The client, in turn, sued Dr. D for malpractice on the grounds that because Dr. D was treating the client at the time the loan was made, Dr. D was engaging in a dual relationship.

The insurance company defended Dr. D, but coverage was limited to defense costs only because claims arising out of any business relationship or venture with any prior or current client of an insured practitioner were excluded from Dr. D's liability coverage. Dr. D was adjudged guilty of malpractice and personally responsible for paying the damages.

The issue in this case is, indeed, one of engaging in a dual relationship. Although Dr. D may have had the best intentions—to support growth in the client—he did not stop to think about the repercussions should the business fail or about the effect such a business relationship would have on the therapeutic relationship. Had Dr. D considered the decision more carefully in relation to the APA *Ethical Principles*, Dr. D might have made another decision. Unfortunately, Dr. D had to pay in more than one way for that decision—the monetary costs of pursuing the repayment suit and paying for the damages in the malpractice suit combined with the potential damage done to Dr. D's professional image, as well as the knowledge that the client might have suffered irreparable harm because of all the trouble.

Example 2: An Industrial/Organizational Psychologist Follows the Rules

Dr. R had worked with the local emergency services department for a number of years, providing evaluations of employees' suitability for promotion within the fire department. Dr. R made sure that all the tests used were up-to-date and appropriate for the individuals tested. Dr. R also maintained careful records on every evaluation performed. Each individual who was evaluated signed a written release describing the nature of the tests Dr. R used and stating that the results of the tests and evaluation would be shared with the fire chief and the director of the emergency services department.

On one occasion, Dr. R performed an evaluation that indicated that a "rising star" in the fire department (who performed very well as an individual and knew all the technical requirements of fire fighting) would not be able to cope with the stresses of managing fire personnel, particularly during emergencies. Dr. R submitted the test and evaluation results to the fire chief and service director, with a recommendation that the employee not be promoted. Shortly thereafter, the employee filed a malpractice suit against Dr. R, claiming that Dr. R had used an inappropriate test and had breached confidentiality.

On receiving the subpoena, Dr. R immediately contacted the insurance company, and the company assigned a lawyer to provide a defense. Dr. R provided appropriate documentation regarding the tests used and copies of the release signed by the employee prior to testing. On the basis of that information, the judge dismissed the case before it went to trial.

Dr. R behaved correctly throughout this incident. Although Dr. R had to experience the stress of being sued, in the end, Dr. R's methodical selection of appropriate tests and careful documentation of the employee's permission to release the results of the tests and evaluation clearly demonstrated that Dr. R had performed correctly.

Example 3: An Argument Among Academic Colleagues Goes Unresolved

University Q received a substantial endowment for doing research on the interactive role of medicine and psychology. The university president set up a committee in the psychology department to develop a plan for doing the research. Before much progress had been made, it became clear that the five committee members were unable to reach an agreement of any kind. In fact, three of them sent a confidential memo to the university president stating that Dr. M was incompetent and requesting that Dr. M be removed from the committee!

Within a few days, after accidentally seeing a copy of the memo, Dr. M filed a suit for slander and libel against the three colleagues. The three colleagues had the same insurance company, which acted to defend them all. The suit was settled before it went to trial.

It is difficult to say why this case was settled out of court. It may be that Dr. M was fully qualified to serve on the committee or that everyone was anxious to avoid the public notice that a suit for libel and defamation would have brought to the university and the department. It may be that it was less costly in time and money to settle the case. Regardless, one wonders whether a lengthier exchange of ideas in a more collegial manner, as advocated in the *Ethical Principles*, might have made it possible to avoid this suit altogether.

Example 4: Supervising a Colleague's Ethical Performance

A number of complaints had been filed claiming that Dr. K used suggestive language when addressing clients, touched them inappropriately, and on at least one occasion had engaged in sexual relations with a client. The ethics committee of the state psychological association investigated the complaints and found them to be valid. The committee censured Dr. K and required Dr. K to practice under the supervision of a colleague for a 2-year period. At the request of the committee, Dr. A was asked to provide regular supervision for Dr. K.

For almost a year, Dr. A provided regular supervision of Dr. K's practice, and Dr. K appeared to be able to avoid inappropriate behavior. So, when Dr. A's mother became ill and Dr. A found it necessary to go out of town for about a month, Dr. A was not particularly concerned about Dr. K's being able to function without active supervision. Dr. A arranged for a colleague to act as Dr. K's emergency contact during that period and gave Dr. K the number.

Some weeks after Dr. A returned to town, several clients filed suit against Dr. K for incidents that had occurred during Dr. A's absence. Dr. K had told neither Dr. A nor Dr. A's stand-in about the incidents. When the clients discovered that Dr. K had no liability insurance, the suit was extended to include Dr. A, charging failure to supervise properly. Dr. A's defense was provided by Dr. A's insurance carrier. The suit was settled out of court.

In this example, Dr. A did what any responsible family member would do under the circumstances: Dr. A went to the aid of his family. The degree to which Dr. A was responsible for taking additional steps, if any, to arrange for Dr. K's supervision is difficult to determine. Dr. A could base decisions related to Dr. K's possible actions during that absence only on what had occurred over the past year. Dr. A assumed that Dr. K would at least use the emergency contact should any incident occur. Of course, Dr. K neither maintained appropriate behavior nor informed either Dr. A or the substitute supervisor of the incidents. As this case demonstrates, supervisory activity always carries special risks.

Example 5: Acting To Protect the Profession

In the past year, Dr. P had served as the academic supervisor for 11 clinical psychology interns, 9 of whom showed great promise as clinical psychologists. Two of the students, however, did not meet the established practice guidelines, as was clearly documented in the records that Dr. P kept. Student A simply was unsuited for clinical work because Student A could not maintain objectivity about the behavior of people whom Student A knew. Student A accepted this critique and moved into another area of specialization. Student B, however, did not accept the critique. Throughout Student B's internship, her academic performance had been very poor, and she did not demonstrate a willingness to learn basic information about important aspects of psychology and about clinical psychology in particular. Student B complained that the criteria applied to others' performance were not as demanding as those applied to hers. Dr. P's personal files reflected Student B's attitude problem, and the grades that she received reflected her lack of academic performance. When the internship period came to a close, Dr. P recommended that Student B not be accepted as a PhD candidate because of poor academic performance, making no mention of her unwillingness to study or her poor attitude. Student B was not accepted as a candidate. When Student B tried to transfer to the program at another university, the bad academic report provided by Dr. P's university prevented acceptance at the second university as well.

Shortly thereafter, Student B filed a suit against Dr. P and the university, alleging that Dr. P had recommended that she not be accepted because of personal dislike, had not reported her academic performance objectively, and had made untrue statements about her in the recommendation. Through the lawyer provided by the insurance carrier, Dr. P provided copies of Student B's records to the court. After seeing the records and hearing testimony from Student B that was intended to prove that Dr. P had inappropriately prevented her from pursuing a career in clinical psychology, the judge determined that there was nothing in the report that reflected personal animosity or that represented slander. The case was dismissed.

Providing accurate reports of a good student's performance is easy, but providing accurate reports of poor performance can be difficult, both because of the potential for inappropriately blocking the student's academic and professional goals and because it is difficult to predict how a student will react. It was clear to Dr. P that Student B was not accepting of criticism or willing to work at the profession and would therefore make a very poor psychologist in any area of specialization. At the same time, Dr. P recognized that the grades Student B received were an effective and objective measure of her abilities. A factual report of those grades indicated that Student B was not right for this field of endeavor without commenting on personal characteristics. Thus it was possible to provide an accurate negative reference both within Dr. P's university and elsewhere.

Example 6: Guarding Against the Possibilities

Dr. W had been treating Client D for severe depression for some time. During recent sessions, Client D had become more and more open in discussing suicide. Late one afternoon, Client D and Client D's spouse appeared unexpectedly at Dr. W's office. Client D's spouse indicated that Client D had actually attempted suicide that morning. Dr. W evaluated Client D and recommended to Client D's spouse that Client D be immediately committed to a psychiatric facility. Client D's spouse became very upset and insisted on taking Client D to their family physician for evaluation. Dr. W tried to convince Client D's spouse to hospitalize Client D in the local facility but did not suggest that there be a consultation between the physician and Dr. W. The physician who evaluated Client D agreed that Client D should be hospitalized for depression, and made the arrangements at the local medical hospital, which had very few staff members trained to handle mentally disturbed patients.

D's admission record and chart noted that Client D was extremely depressed and should be monitored carefully because of a history of suicidal symptoms but did not mention the failed suicide attempt. On the evening of Client D's admission, during the shift change when the night nursing staff came on and no one was observing, Client D committed suicide. Client D's spouse sued the hospital, the family physician, and Dr. W for malpractice.

When the suit came to trial, the jury found all three parties named in the suit guilty of malpractice, with the hospital bearing a significant portion of the guilt because of the inattentiveness of staff and the lack of qualified staff to oversee Client D's treatment. Dr. W and the family physician were held negligent for failing to convey the severity of Client D's condition. The hospital paid the greatest part of the liability damages.

Note that the requirement to provide correctly trained and attentive staff to supervise Client D was considered to be the most important consideration. However, Dr. W's failure to consult with the family physician appears to have contributed to the lack of understanding about the severity of Client D's condition.

Example 7: Maintaining Confidentiality Extends to One's Colleagues as Well

Dr. B, a psychologist and a newly appointed member of the state psychological association's ethics committee, was somewhat amazed by some of the complaints that had been brought against psychologists in the brief time that Dr. B had been on the committee. During a casual dinner with friends, two of whom (Dr. L and Dr. H) were also psychologists, Dr. B and the psychologists started talking about ethics in general. Although Dr. B was well aware of the prohibition against discussing any aspect of the complaints heard by the ethics committee, Dr. B discussed several cases in general terms to illustrate points in the discussion. The details of one case were sufficient to make it clear to Dr. L and Dr. H that a particular psychologist who practiced in the city, Dr. V, was the psychologist involved in the complaint. Within a few days, it became common knowledge throughout the community that Dr. V had been charged with and found guilty of an ethics violation.

Shortly thereafter, Dr. V lodged a complaint with the ethics committee regarding the breach of confidentiality. An investigation revealed that the source of the leak had been Dr. B. Accompanied by a lawyer (not provided by Dr. B's insurance carrier because there was no civil suit involved), Dr. B testified before the committee, admitting to discussing the case but explaining that he had tried to remove all identifying information while doing so. The committee censured Dr. B, noting that any discussion, even one in general terms, violated ethical standards.

Discussion of ethics and practice guidelines is one of the ways in which one's understanding of them is increased. However, Dr. B had privileged information and was ethically bound not to discuss, outside of official functions, any aspect of the complaints heard by the ethics committee. Note that the insurance carrier did not provide Dr. B with a lawyer. Liability insurance typically does not cover actions that are not civil suits.

Example 8: When Is "Expert Testimony" Really Expert?

> The defense attorney for a convicted rapist asked Dr. E to evaluate the convicted man's degree of dangerousness, pending a decision by the court about whether to grant the defendant a few days of supervised freedom to settle personal affairs. Dr. E evaluated the man and testified that he did not appear to pose a threat to the community at that time. The judge sentenced the man to prison for the rape but then granted the man 7 days of supervised freedom in which to settle his affairs prior to initiation of the jail term. During that period, the man raped several other women. One of the rape victims filed suit against Dr. E, claiming that Dr. E had failed to evaluate the man correctly. Dr. E provided documentation of the procedures followed. In the end, because the jury held that the court had been responsible for the man's release, they brought a judgment of no liability for Dr. E.

The judgment resulted from a jury's decision that the court did not have to agree with Dr. E's evaluation and chose to release the convicted rapist. The question of the accuracy of Dr. E's evaluation was not reviewed per se. Although Dr. E was not held responsible in legal terms, it would be advisable for Dr. E to review the method and results of the evaluation.

Example 9: Handling Emergencies

> Late one evening, when Dr. T was on call at the local hospital, two people were brought into the emergency room by the police and an ambulance crew. One of the people was severely injured due to a beating administered by the other, and the medical staff immediately admitted the injured person into the hospital. The person who had committed the assault was still extremely violent. Dr. T, in consultation with the medical staff, evaluated the individual, determining that involuntary commitment to the psychiatric ward would be appropriate pending further evaluation. All actions taken by Dr. T and the hospital were carefully documented.
>
> Within 24 hours, the person who committed the assault was found to have been in a drug-induced psychotic state. Appropriate medication relieved the condition, and the individual was released. The individual then filed suit against Dr. T and the hospital on the grounds that they had violated the plaintiff's civil rights. Dr. T's insurance carrier provided a defense lawyer for Dr. T, through whom Dr. T

provided personal records of the commitment. After reviewing both Dr. T's records and the hospital's records of the commitment, the court found that Dr. T and the hospital had acted according to the best standards of care and dismissed the suit.

Handling emergency evaluations is a stressful, sometimes confusing task. However, by following established procedures and keeping in mind that the future welfare of the person experiencing difficulties and of others depends on the actions taken, Dr. T and the hospital staff acted correctly. In this instance, correct documentation was the key to the decision made by the court.

Example 10: Protecting Users From Harm

Dr. N, a psychologist, was asked by a publisher to prepare a series of videotapes on the relation of exercise, good physical health, and good mental health. Working with Dr. O, a physician colleague with expertise in exercise, Dr. N prepared a series of seven tapes. The tapes included recommended exercise programs. Each tape also included a warning that no one should use the tapes without first obtaining a physical examination from a qualified physician and that certain individuals (e.g., those with a history of angina) should not engage in any exercise program unless they did so under the supervision of their physician.

Buyer F, who was overweight, purchased one of the tapes and began the exercise program without following the recommendation that a physical examination be obtained first. Buyer F suffered a heart attack during exercising and subsequently instituted a suit against Dr. N and Dr. O, claiming incorrect treatment that resulted in bodily injury. Dr. N was defended in the suit by a lawyer provided by the carrier of Dr. N's liability insurance. After hearing the tapes and other testimony, the jury decided that neither Dr. N nor Dr. O were responsible for Buyer F's heart attack because Buyer F failed to heed the warning included in the tapes.

In this instance, Dr. N took steps to insure that the well-being of users was protected. Dr. N relied on the expert advice of a physician and made sure that potential users would be aware not only of the benefits but also of the risks of the procedures described.

In Closing

These ten examples demonstrate both the variety of roles that psychologists can play and the nature of some of the problems that they may face. In many instances, the insurance carrier acted on behalf of the psychologist. In one or two instances, the nature of the complaint meant that the psychologist had to act without the advice of the carrier or the protection of insurance.

Almost any professional situation, if not properly handled or if it leads to injury or damage (real or perceived), may result in malpractice litigation. A psychologist can be sued by anyone for any reason at any time. But there are safeguards that help protect psychologists from frivolous suits. For example, a psychologist may recover attorney's fees from a plaintiff or a plaintiff's attorney, or may benefit from early motions to dismiss. Respectable attorneys, working under contingency fee arrangements, will have little incentive to invest their own time, energy, and resources in a suit that is clearly without foundation.

The remainder of this volume provides an explanation of what constitutes professional liability, raises questions that may be useful in evaluating ways to perform one's duties as a psychologist, and provides an explanation of the functions and limitations of professional liability insurance (PLI).

2

Practice Guidelines and Ethics: What Do They Really Mean?

A set of practices and implicitly recognized principles of conduct evolve over the history of every profession. Such principles guide the relationships of the members of the profession to their users, to each other, and to the community. Making such guiding principles and practices explicit is a sign of the profession's maturity and serves the best interests of the profession, its users, and the community at large.

Because psychology is a continually evolving science and profession, guidelines for practice are living documents.

There is a tendency to write and speak about practice guidelines and ethics as if both were matters of concern only to philosophers and theorists, or as if their application were the province of saints. However, practice guidelines and ethics are developed in response to the practical concerns of people who work in a profession and people who use the services provided by the profession. As such, they represent practical tools that can be used to shape the way in which a person practices that profession. And, like all tools, each standard, principle, or guideline may work better under one circumstance than under another. Moreover, as time passes and circumstances change, a new or better standard, principle, or guideline must be developed to meet changing needs.

This chapter discusses how professional practice guidelines and ethics for psychologists differ from laws and regulations governing practice as well as the relation of those practice guidelines and ethics to other professions. It also discusses how the *Ethical Principles of Psychologists, General Guidelines for Providers of Psychological Services* (APA Board of Professional Affairs, 1987), and similar documents can guide psychologists in their daily practice.

What Is Meant by Principles, Standards, and Guidelines?

For the purpose of discussion in this volume, *ethics* are theories or systems of moral principles that provide a code of conduct. Each *principle* within an ethical system is a rule that fulfills the intent of the code, sometimes specific (e.g., "Thou shalt not murder"); and sometimes general (e.g., "In providing services, psychologists maintain the highest standards of their profession").

A *standard* of performance or conduct is an act or pattern of action that is accepted—by custom or by some authority—as a model or example of action that fulfills the intent of a principle within a code of ethics.

A *guideline* is an outline or summary of actions or procedures one may use in order to work at the level of performance established as the standard of performance under that principle.

At each level of development, ethics provide a goal to be reached, however difficult it may be to do so. Understanding these concepts allows one to put psychology's ethics into perspective. The *Ethical Principles of Psychologists* is a code of conduct (an ethical system) formulated by a select group of psychologists, based on their experience in the field, passed by the American Psychological Association (APA) Council of Representatives, and acknowledged and accepted (through the act of joining the APA) by psychologists who are members of the APA. Psychologists who are members of the APA must conduct themselves according to the *Ethical Principles*, and many psychologists who are not APA members follow the *Ethical Principles* either by choice or because an authority other than the APA requires them to do so.[1]

Depending on a psychologist's area of specialty, some of the principles may not have a great impact, and others may require constant consideration. Psychologists have developed guidelines for help in following these models, such as the *General Guidelines for Providers of Psychological Services* and the *Specialty Guidelines for the Delivery of Services* (APA Board of Professional Affairs, 1981), as well as other collections of practical guidelines that can be used in daily practice.

How Psychology Establishes Ethical Principles, Standards, and Guidelines

Psychology was a working discipline for many years before the members of the APA began the process of formally codifying the principles and practice guidelines that underlie professional psychology today. The foundation of the discipline, which rests on understanding and improving the lives of individuals, engendered high standards of conduct from the outset.

Psychologists working as researchers, educators, and practitioners in a variety of settings were expected to behave in a manner that conformed to the guidelines and ethics applied to others working in those settings. At the same time, the nature of the work (e.g., research) that psychologists did required that new or different practice guidelines be developed that would assure a high quality of training and conduct specific to psychologists. For example, while employing research methods developed in the "hard" sciences, psychologists devised accompanying practice guidelines better suited to psychological research. This process is still going on today.

Not until the 1930s did APA members create a committee with the primary goals of (a) assessing the nature of ethics and practice guidelines within the discipline as applied by APA members; (b) improving professional practice guidelines

---

[1]Many state statutes regulating psychology incorporate the *Ethical Principles* or similar codes of ethics as guiding principles to regulate the conduct of licensed and certified psychologists.

through education; and (c) providing a means for disciplining those members who did not meet articulated, but as yet informal, ethics and practice guidelines of the discipline.

In the early 1950s, as the stature of the profession increased and membership in the APA began to grow, members recognized the need for setting out practice guidelines and ethics for themselves and their colleagues to meet. The first effort to codify what are now the *Ethical Principles of Psychologists* was then made.

As individual specialties have become more defined, the need for other sets of guidelines supporting and expanding upon the *Ethical Principles* has been recognized, and various guidelines (e.g., *General Guidelines for Providers of Psychological Services* and *Specialty Guidelines for the Delivery of Services*) have been developed, based on the *Ethical Principles* and accepted practice guidelines of the profession. Such guidelines are intended to provide psychologists with advice on how to apply the *Ethical Principles* and other practice guidelines in a practical way.

Today, the *Ethical Principles* form the foundation of ethical performance for psychologists regardless of their specialty or setting of practice. Keeping the *Ethical Principles* up-to-date is a process of consensus and referendum that involves the entire membership. Applying for and accepting membership in the APA entails accepting the requirement that, as a member, a psychologist must conduct himself or herself in a manner consistent with the *Ethical Principles* and that to do otherwise violates the basic standards established for the profession.

Although the *Ethical Principles* and other practice guidelines guide the performance of APA members, psychologists who are not members of the APA are not compelled to adhere to the same standards unless the APA principles and standards have been adopted into federal, state, or local laws or regulations governing their practice. The APA *Ethical Principles* (or other APA guidelines) have been incorporated into most state statutes regulating the practice of psychology. Regardless, most psychologists who are not members of the APA choose to adhere to the principles and standards of the APA and its members because they accept them as the basic standards that must be met by true professionals.

Enforcement Within the APA

The APA Ethics Committee is the body within the APA that oversees ethical matters. The Ethics Committee is made up of members who are (a) known and respected for their understanding of and dedication to the ethics of the profession; (b) nominated from among the broad membership; (c) approved by both the Ethics Committee and the Board of Directors; and (d) elected by the Council of Representatives. The objectives of the committee include:

- Formulating principles of ethics for adoption by the association;
- Receiving and investigating complaints of unethical conduct of fellows, members, and associates;
- Resolving complaints of unethical conduct or recommending

such other action as is necessary to achieve the objectives of the association;

  • Reporting on types of complaints investigated with special description of difficult or recalcitrant cases; and

  • Adopting rules and procedures governing the conduct of the committee.

The fundamental objectives of the committee shall be to maintain ethical conduct by psychologists at the highest professional level, to educate psychologists concerning ethical principles, to protect those members of the public with whom psychologists have a professional or scientific relationship, and to aid the association in achieving its objectives as reflected in its bylaws.

Although the committee shall endeavor to take actions toward members found to be in violation of the APA *Ethical Principles* that are educative and constructive rather than punitive in character, the committee's primary concern will be to protect the public against harmful conduct by psychologists. (APA Ethics Committee, 1985, p. 685)

The APA Ethics Office accepts formal complaints against individual members of the APA from both members and nonmembers. In addition, the committee may initiate a complaint against a member from materials in the public domain. The committee, following an investigation of a complaint against a member, can dismiss the complaint as having no significant substance (with or without an educative letter), issue a sanction, or recommend to the Board of Directors that a complainee be allowed to resign membership under stipulated conditions or that a complainee be dropped from membership. Once the Board of Directors votes to drop a member, the membership is notified of that action. In cases where the individual is allowed to resign membership, only the Council of Representatives is notified.

Additional Sources of Peer Review

Peer review related to ethics and standards can be formal or informal. Ethics committees of state and local psychological associations, peer review groups associated with certification and licensing boards, and peer review boards used by insurance carriers and other groups also act to determine whether a psychologist is practicing according to the established standards of the profession. Such groups are made up of psychologists and other mental health professionals who, at least theoretically, understand the concerns and methods of psychologists and respect the needs of those whom psychologists are treating or to whom they provide other services.

State and local association ethics committees examine complaints and recommend when and if a psychologist should be disciplined by those groups. Peer review boards associated with certification and license boards are primarily concerned with assuring that an individual practices in a manner consistent with the requirements of the state or locality. Licensing boards are empowered to deny, suspend, place on probation, or revoke licenses. Generally, this requires that they base their judgments on the accepted principles and standards of practice within their state or locality, and those standards and principles may or may not take into consideration the accepted APA *Ethical Principles* and practice guidelines.

Peer review boards associated with insurance carriers may include psychologists but are not necessarily required to do so. Such boards have the responsibility of reviewing claims filed for psychological services and determining whether the claims are for appropriate treatments (usually based on some kind of accepted practice guidelines) and, if so, whether insurance coverage is applicable according to the terms of the insurance policy.

Another source of peer review may be found in clinics, hospitals, and group practices. Peer review groups in such settings are formed for the express purposes of reviewing how individual cases are handled; making recommendations on assessment, treatment, and so forth; and assuring that quality guidelines are met. Peer review boards in work settings may also make recommendations regarding the hiring or dismissing of psychologists.

Finally, when a difficult case arises, a psychologist's colleagues can act as peer reviewers by providing advice on how treatment might be handled. Many psychologists form peer consultation groups to seek consultation related to difficult cases. Such a peer group can be useful in keeping one up-to-date in the field and, of course, can be a source of role models. It may also be useful for a psychologist to undergo therapy to deal with daily stresses or special circumstances that arise; one's peers can provide this therapy.

The Individual Psychologist

Ultimately, it is the responsibility of each psychologist to uphold the accepted practice guidelines and principles that determine the level of ethical practice within the profession. Dedicated psychologists make an intense effort to maintain and enlarge their knowledge of the discipline and to develop the methods and skills necessary to apply that knowledge. Moreover, they make a conscious effort to uphold the guidelines for ethical practice. Understanding the many levels of the formal and, in some cases, informal professional codes is a challenge, especially because each principle and practice guideline must be considered in relation to many local, state, and federal rules and regulations.

How Do APA Principles, Standards, and Guidelines Relate to Laws and Regulations?

Because the APA is the largest professional body representing psychologists and is one of the most prestigious professional bodies within the mental health disciplines, the APA's *Ethical Principles* and other professional practice guidelines are respected by other professional and legal bodies. The APA practice guidelines are used as models by other professions and organizations seeking to develop similar codes and are frequently taken into consideration when laws and regulations are being developed that may govern the practice of psychology and other mental health disciplines.

Outside of the association, the legal standing of the APA *Ethical Principles* (and standards and guidelines supporting those principles) is determined by whether part or all of them have been incorporated into laws and regulations and, if so, which form that incorporation has taken. Laws are codified (by local, state, or federal legislative bodies) in order to protect society as a whole or individuals within society or to legitimatize actions taken on behalf of or toward society or its members.

If an agency or department of government is given the task of enforcing a law, that agency or department develops sets of rules, called regulations, that provide practical means of enforcing the law. The agency usually does this on its own, sometimes with input from legislators and sometimes, but by no means always, with input from individuals who understand the practical implications of a law.

Psychologists are affected by laws and regulations at all levels and, whether they are members of APA or not, the APA *Ethical Principles* and the standards and guidelines derived from them have a significant impact on their practice. In most states, the *Ethical Principles* and accepted standards of practice have been incorporated into laws or regulations that set out requirements for certification or licensure. Some states have consumer laws that expressly govern mental health practice and incorporate either the APA *Ethical Principles* or similar concepts. Agencies that enforce the laws have included them in enforcement regulations. In other words, upholding the profession's ethics and practice guidelines invests the psychologist with credentials. This, in turn, has legal implications in relation to professional liability. Thus, following the *Ethical Principles* and practice guidelines of the profession is vital, not only in philosophical terms but also in legal terms.

What Happens When Ethics and the Law Are in Conflict?

The potential for conflict between the principles and practice guidelines of psychology and the law (local, state, and federal) is ever-present. In some instances, laws (and the regulations that aid in their implementation) may be written in a way that does not take into account the nuances or the complexities of psychological practice. In other instances, the standards that are incorporated into some laws are more appropriate for another profession or set of concerns. Take these two instances:

• The regulations governing how to file insurance claims may require a psychologist to give a detailed explanation of the need for treatment and of the treatment itself. Conflicts may arise in determining what a "detailed" explanation consists of and what appropriate treatment may be, in addition to conflicts involving the breaching of confidentiality. Depending on what is revealed, the insurance claim or coverage in general may be rejected.

• It may be possible to commit someone to a mental institution without psychological evaluation, based on the recommendation of a physician because the person's condition has become unmanageable in a medical hospital setting. This can be done regardless of whether the patient's behavior results from a psychological disorder or from a medical disorder.

In some instances, the law may raise questions about possible limits on the *Ethical Principles* and practice guidelines of psychology. For example, what should a psychologist do if a client who is diagnosed as having AIDS or is tested positive for HIV reveals that he or she is continuing to engage in sexual relations without concern for "safe sex" practices and without telling his or her partners? If the client gives the actual names of partners, does the psychologist's duty to protect others extend to those partners? Does case law (that is, decisions in actual cases) indicate that the psychologist has a legal obligation to warn them (remembering that there are no federal or state laws requiring reporting such instances at this time)?

Under circumstances such as these, and in circumstances that are less dramatic, the degree of the psychologist's understanding of and ability to evaluate professional principles and practice guidelines as well as the laws governing practice, concern for the client, and the circumstances must be examined in resolving *to his or her satisfaction* what should be done. In other words, the psychologist must use his or her sense of judgment about the issues and concerns inherent in a particular situation.

Of course, no matter how reasonable and fair a legal requirement may be and how able the psychologist may be in balancing all considerations, there will be times when this type of dilemma cannot be resolved to everyone's satisfaction. The psychologist may act in ways that appear to violate a client's rights (as when a psychologist warns a potential victim of a client's violent intentions) or in ways that place the psychologist in direct defiance of the law (as when a psychologist's records are subpoenaed in a divorce case and he or she refuses to provide copies of personal notes about one partner when both were treated during couples therapy). The psychologist has the responsibility of weighing all sides of the question and resolving the dilemma in a way that, in his or her best judgment, upholds the principles and practice guidelines of the profession.

Regardless of the circumstances surrounding a suit, the laws that permit such suits are for the protection of all who interact within and with the profession. Psychologists must conduct themselves in such a way that will conform both to the ethics and practice guidelines of the profession and to the law, and they must be prepared for those instances when conflicts arise. Psychologists may also work to change the laws so that such conflicts do not occur.

Resources for the Psychologist in a Dilemma

The psychologist's most important resources are knowledge of psychology, a belief in and understanding of the *Ethical Principles* and similar guidelines, and a clear understanding of his or her abilities and limitations as a psychologist. The psychologist needs to know how ethical principles and practice guidelines have been applied by the APA Ethics Committee and similar bodies.[2]

---

[2]Reports of such decisions are often published in the *American Psychologist* and other professional publications, and the *Casebook on Ethical Principles of Psychologists* (APA, 1990) is a particularly valuable source for examples.

It is also valuable for a psychologist to have a good understanding of laws related to practice, consumer rights, and similar matters. Some questions can be resolved only in relation to legal statutes and regulations. Knowledge of local and state court rulings as well as federal court rulings is also important because such rulings establish precedents for future actions by courts and provide a foundation for future laws and regulations.

Knowledge of the profession and of how its rules are applied both in professional and legal settings is essential for the psychologist, who must understand the dilemmas that arise and must resolve most, but not all, conflicts. A psychologist's peers may be able to provide insight. Local, state, and national organizations (such as the APA and the APA Ethics Office) are also excellent resources when information on standards of practice and alternatives for resolving conflict are needed.[3]

The better informed a psychologist is and the more he or she knows about the resources that are available, the more likely it is that the psychologist will be able to resolve a conflict satisfactorily, at least in his or her own mind.

Competence

Being a competent professional means having the knowledge, skills, and abilities necessary to perform a constellation of tasks relevant to that profession as well as understanding when it is appropriate to provide services or to refer a client. The more demanding a profession is, the greater the knowledge and number of skills and abilities that will be required and the more likely it will be that a professional will not be competent to provide services in all areas of the profession. This is as true for psychology as it is for any other discipline.

A psychologist must be competent to assess the foundation and motivation for behavior, to evaluate the ways in which that behavior needs to change, and to provide the guidance needed to effect that change. A psychologist's competence is derived from personal ability, understanding of self, formal training, and continuing education. A psychologist needs to have good people skills, including an enjoyment of interacting with others, patience, and good verbal skills. A psychologist must be able to be objective, about his or her own behavior as well as that of others, and to analyze behavior and motivations in order to gain perspective. A good psychologist evaluates personal motivations and works toward self-understanding in order to be able to support the needs of people seeking his or her services.

Formal training is gained at the undergraduate and graduate levels of study. Undergraduate study and master's-level study provide a foundation of knowledge needed for understanding what will be learned in later study and provide some of the skills necessary for research and practice. It is at the doctoral level that a psychologist builds the substantial specific knowledge and skills required to be effective in a particular area of practice. Doctoral programs, coupled with supervised field and intern experience, are the first major phase of a psychologist's development in becoming a true professional.

---

[3]Part II of this volume provides a collection of points to consider that may be useful in decision making and in avoiding and resolving conflicts.

Once a psychologist begins to practice, both experience and continuing education become the primary means for enlarging skills and for becoming more effective. Continuing education may take many forms, including postgraduate training at a university, continuing education courses taught by qualified professionals in the field, keeping abreast of current literature, and obtaining supervised experience.

State licensing or certification requirements, or both determine whether one can initially obtain a license to practice. Such requirements vary greatly from one state to another. It is the responsibility of each applicant to contact the state, to obtain guidelines on what is required, and to ask questions if there is any confusion. Moreover, if maintaining a license is contingent on demonstrating continued competence through continuing education or another means or on performing other tasks (e.g., additional in-service training), the psychologist must be prepared to meet those requirements and must periodically document their fulfillment.

Inadvertent failure to provide accurate information or meet a requirement at any time is not usually a significant matter. Taking corrective steps or obtaining an extension for meeting a requirement may be possible. However, deliberately falsifying data or in some other way misrepresenting competence is at the least unethical and in some states, in fact, may be a crime.

Having a strong belief in a particular methodology or way of life can strengthen one's competence to practice. However, one's beliefs and attitudes may begin to overshadow objectivity, and one may need to step back and reevaluate how one is providing services. Self-care and self-awareness are two of the competent psychologist's most valuable tools. Personal beliefs and attitudes, physical and emotional fatigue, personal problems, and other concerns of the psychologist can dramatically affect how he or she provides services. If a psychologist is unable to view a patient's concerns objectively, the effectiveness of the psychologist's decision making can be reduced. He or she may even do more harm than good. A competent psychologist maintains his or her well-being by seeking physical and psychological care when it is needed, by being alert to the signs of stress and burnout, and by evaluating the decisions he or she has made in relation to the needs of his or her clients.

Another element of competence is knowing which services and treatments should be provided by other professionals and knowing who can provide those services. Such services might include additional assessment, focused psychological treatment with which the referring psychologist has limited or no experience, or medical treatment.

Psychologists cannot provide every service needed by every client. If a psychologist is going to recommend that a service be provided by another professional, he or she should understand enough about the services required to provide an appropriate referral or to provide guidance on how to find those services and should be able to help the client understand what to expect from the professional providing the service. This does not mean, for example, that the psychologist has to know all the nuances of a medical treatment, but it does mean that he or she has a responsibility to understand the implications of what is involved. And when providing the names of individuals who might provide the service, the psychologist should know the professional qualifications of the person being recommended.

If a psychologist wishes to provide a new or different kind of service, that is, to enlarge his or her competence, it is expected that he or she will obtain additional postgraduate training (either from a university-based program, in the form of continuing education, or through supervised experience) that will provide him or her with the minimum knowledge and skills necessary to provide those services ethically.

Peer consultation is one of the most important resources for maintaining and enlarging competence. Within the limits of confidentiality, discussing a specific concern with more experienced colleagues about how one should provide a service can help clarify what action to take and will help resolve personal conflict. Peer consultation sharpens one's professional skills by challenging one's ability to explain the concern, providing a different viewpoint and the benefit of other psychologists' experiences, and in some circumstances, providing an opportunity to correct treatment errors before a client is harmed.

Formal peer consultation in treatment settings such as clinics serves much the same function and helps maintain the standard of care. For example, when a psychologist is told that a claim for services has been questioned or rejected, the psychologist may need only to improve his or her skill in how to file a claim and explain treatment. However, if the claim is questioned because the treatment may be inappropriate, the psychologist may need to examine his or her method of treatment.

Thus, competence involves not only knowing and understanding a body of knowledge and the ways in which methods and techniques can be used but also having good judgment about one's own character and capacities and those of other psychologists. It also means accepting the responsibility for maintaining both skills and well-being. To the degree that a psychologist does not have the level of competence required to perform as a professional, he or she may do harm to those seeking services. To the degree that he or she is willing to enlarge and enhance competence, he or she will be better able to meet the needs of the profession and the client.

Psychologists as professionals have another responsibility—to monitor their colleagues' competency to practice. This may seem presumptuous or even inappropriate to some, but being aware of the competence of one's colleagues allows one to identify when a psychologist or other mental health professional is not providing the services he or she claims to provide in an appropriate manner. Inadequate or harmful service provided by one professional can do harm to the image and valuation of the profession as a whole and, of paramount importance, may harm the consumers of those services. When such abuses come to light, it may be possible to correct them through peer pressure (e.g., offering a colleague critique and support and obtaining his or her cooperation). However, the duty and responsibility of an ethical psychologist is to eliminate that abuse even if it becomes necessary to file a complaint against that person with the licensing board, or with the APA, or both. It may even become necessary to assist in bringing civil or criminal charges against that person.

Confidentiality

In theory, the concept of confidentiality is straightforward: An ethical psychologist does not discuss or provide details about a client in any form without the express permission of that individual. In reality, however, maintaining complete confidentiality may be impossible in some situations. Both the needs of the client and the appropriate needs of others must be met.

It is the responsibility of the psychologist providing clinical psychology services to make sure that each client understands the course of treatment, including the roles that the psychologist, the client, and others may play in that treatment and the nature of records that will be kept as well as how those records will or may be used.

If the psychologist must share information about a client, the question of how much to share will arise. It may be impossible to obtain specific consent from each client every time the need to consult arises. It is also unrealistic to expect that a general consent can be given because some information may not fall into the categories that such a consent is intended to release. Some settings, such as public and hospital clinics, may require the psychologist to discuss each patient with one or more colleagues or even with a committee. Thus, the psychologist must use sound judgment in determining what information will be shared not only with the patient but also with colleagues.

Another concern is the nature of record keeping. Psychologists maintain records on their clients, including treatment records and records of evaluations. In some settings, such as clinics, data derived from records also play a part in quality control, cost evaluation, and cost assessment. And of course, some information must be reported when insurance claims are made.

At any time, demands for more information than one is willing to provide may be made. Thus, questions will arise about which information can be shared without violating a patient's right to confidentiality and about how to provide even confidential information in order to best serve the client's needs.

An equally important question is how to enter information in a record not only so that one has the information required to support the patient's treatment but also so that one provides the information needed to fulfill the reporting requirements of insurance companies, government agencies, elements of the legal system, and other entities to whom the psychologist has some obligation. This is one of the greatest challenges a psychologist faces. As long as the information that can be shared can be easily sorted out from the client's file, there is no conflict. However, it is becoming increasingly difficult to meet all requirements and still maintain appropriate confidentiality. Moreover, it is not possible to predict when or under what circumstances demands will be made that records be shared. And there are statutory exceptions to confidentiality or privileged communication, such as in child-abuse reporting laws, court-ordered evaluations, and civil commitment proceedings.

Record-keeping practices must be learned and guidelines established that can be followed in developing files. If the guidelines are carefully and ethically thought out, it is more likely that the client's right to confidentiality can be maintained and the needs for reporting can be accommodated.

Conflict may arise even in the treatment setting itself. For example, how much feedback and analysis can be provided to an individual client when more than one person is being treated in each session? Group and family therapy involve close interaction during each session. How much of what the psychologist learns is relevant to the therapy of others in the session? In couples therapy, how much (if any) information about one partner gained in an individual session can be appropriately shared with the other partner during a joint session? Can a psychologist ethically discuss such information with only one of the partners?

When a client's behavior is illegal or when the client is a threat to others, the psychologist is faced with the dilemma of determining what action he or she should take to protect the well-being of others and to comply with the law. Some states have laws that define the psychologist's responsibility. For example, some states require that if a client tells a psychologist that he or she is going to commit a crime and indicates when and how the crime will be committed and who the victim will be, the psychologist must report that information to the authorities. Thus a limit is placed on the degree to which a client can be protected against self-disclosure. However, the psychologist must still evaluate the reality of the threat and the client's ability to follow through with it. The psychologist must determine at what point his or her duty to the client (and need to maintain the client's trust in order to provide effective treatment) is superseded by the moral and legal duty to warn others and society of the client's potential to do harm.

Protecting the rights of those deemed incompetent or those who depend upon one for protection because they are vulnerable is an important responsibility. If a client is unable to act in his or her own best interest due to illness or if he or she is vulnerable because of age (as in the case of minors), incapacity (as in the case of the elderly who are incompetent), or circumstance (as in the case of a prisoner), the psychologist must protect the rights of that individual from invasion of privacy or, to the extent possible, from the loss of autonomy and self-determination. Parents, government agencies, courts, schools, insurance companies, and others in positions of authority may make demands for details of treatment, as well as copies of tests and test results without appropriate interpretations.

At times, the client's well-being may be fostered by sharing information. At other times, however, information that is requested may not be relevant to the purpose for which it is being requested, or sharing it may violate the client's right to protection against self-disclosure or other rights. The psychologist becomes the guardian of the rights of his or her clients and of others with whom he or she may interact as a psychologist.

Assessment Techniques

Having appropriate knowledge of and competence to use assessment techniques is key to a psychologist's ability to practice. It is the psychologist's responsibility to understand the applications and limitations of assessment techniques, including how those techniques address the needs of ethnic minorities and other specific groups. Understanding that what may be appropriate for use with one individual may not be appropriate for use with another individual means having a full understanding of the structure of each tool and of its validity. It also means understanding the limitations of one's own ability to administer the tool and to evaluate the results.

Some individuals, particularly those who are not trained, look upon assessment and assessment tools as finely honed techniques that can provide finite answers to questions about what a person is like, why he or she acts the way he or she does, and what he or she is likely to do in the future. A responsible psychologist understands that this is not the case and knows that assessment is vulnerable not only to misuse and misinterpretation by the untrained but also by psychologists and other professionals.

Therefore the responsible psychologist makes every effort to assure that assessment is conducted in an appropriate manner, with appropriate tools, and under appropriate circumstances. He or she also protects individual rights by maintaining the principle of confidentiality when possible and by assuring that the assessment results will be used correctly.

Because some people expect that assessment will provide a clear picture of what will occur, they believe that assessment will lead to a clear course of action for the psychologist and for them. In a number of settings, such as hospitals, schools, and courts, individuals who request assessment may have little or no understanding of what assessment really means and what the results will be. Their need for precise answers to questions such as how to educate a student who seems to choose not to learn or how to predict behavior leads them to put inordinate pressure to provide those answers on the individuals conducting assessments. Psychologists working in such settings are often faced with the need to educate their supervisors or those who request their services. At times, the effort to educate is difficult or unsuccessful. Thus, both the pressure associated with assessment and the likelihood of being misunderstood—as well as the psychologist's own desire to succeed at the task and to resolve the questions he or she is being asked to answer— can create a conflict for the psychologist. The psychologist must accept the fact that such conflicts may arise and must be prepared to work with others to clarify the role of assessment and its outcome. Above all, the psychologist must be realistic about both the deficiencies and values of assessment.

In Closing

The remaining portions of this volume are dedicated to providing a practical perspective on how the *Ethical Principles* and practice guidelines operate in the often confusing world of daily practice. As you read and consider the discussions and review the focus points set out in Part II of the volume, remember that there are no perfect guidelines, few absolutes, no infallible procedures that can govern practice. However, working according to the *Ethical Principles* and established practice guidelines for the field will carry you a long way toward living up to the highest aims of the profession.

3

What Is Professional Liability?

This chapter provides a framework for understanding a subject about which psychologists may not be fully informed—the present legal structure as it relates to professional liability. This framework not only catalogs currently applicable facts about the matter but also provides information that should be useful even if the law and insurance environments change.

This chapter concerns malpractice proper, which is classified in law as an *unintentional tort* (see p. 34). *Intentional torts* such as breach of contract (see p. 36; see also pp. 51, 54), lawsuits arising out of other disputes, and areas where practitioners could face criminal charges are also areas of potential liability that are briefly discussed in chapter 5 in the section, Policy Exclusions: Where Are You Left Unprotected? (See p. 113.)

Professional Liability: Key Concepts

- Because psychologists by legal tradition are professionals, they can be sued for malpractice when accused of negligence.

- The judgment of the court regarding who, if anyone, is responsible for what actions (and the extent of liability for monetary damages) will depend on whether a legal case can be proven, according to the rules and precedents that are established in a particular state's judicial system.

- The legal system imposes a specific and predictable formula for the prosecution of malpractice suits. When a psychologist is sued, all parties must play by these rules.

- APAIT data indicate that the probability of a psychologist being sued is extremely small (less than half of 1%), and the average cost of a claim is under $22,000.

- Nonetheless, there appear to be sound reasons to maintain professional liability insurance throughout one's professional career and perhaps beyond.

- The private insurance industry provides protection against malpractice through errors and omissions policies that cover most acts of negligence.

- Practitioners need to understand the limits of their insurance coverage in order to know which situations may not be protected by insurance.

Why Should You Be Concerned *Now* About Professional Liability and the Law?

Fortunately, most psychologists do their best to practice ethically and effectively and to comply with the local, state, and federal laws that govern psychological practice. And most psychologists wisely buy liability insurance to protect their personal assets in the event of a malpractice suit. There are, however, at least three good reasons why practitioners should be concerned about these issues.

First, it is usually only when a subpoena arrives at the psychologist's door (or the door of a colleague) that he or she begins to consider what can happen if a suit is filed. A threat or notice of an actual suit is extremely stressful. At these times, it is not uncommon for a practitioner to be upset, confused, and impatient. Thus, the effectiveness with which he or she may deal with a suit can be limited. The more you know and learn now, the less confusing and stressful such a situation will be and the more effective your response can be.

Second, and more important, a knowledgeable professional will be able to integrate actual information about insurance and the law into clinical decision making. No practitioner should undertake to practice without first understanding the legal and insurance gestalt that surrounds that practice.

Third, and finally, one must recognize that malpractice claims arise against not only dishonorable practitioners but also against honorable practitioners who unknowingly open a window of legal vulnerability through their actions or inactions. As those experienced with the human side of malpractice emphasize again and again, *the best way to avoid being sued or to protect oneself in the event of a claim is to know the rules.* If you don't know those rules or have forgotten them, this volume offers you the opportunity to learn or review them.

The Practitioner and the Law

Civil law is composed of both written and statutory law. Statutory law consists of precedents interpreting written law in relation to a particular case and of judges' rulings. Over the years, civil law polishes the mirror into which society looks to see what *civilized* people expect from one another. That is, civil law is in a constant state of modification, reflecting changes in people's needs and expectations and in society's conditions. When this code of rules and principles appears to have been violated, the person who claims to have been harmed (the plaintiff) can bring a lawsuit for malpractice (and monetary damages) against the alleged offender (the defendant), who then must answer the accusation. Unless the plaintiff's claim can be quickly disproved or the plaintiff can be persuaded to drop the suit, perhaps in exchange for a monetary settlement, a trial is convened during which the relevant standards of civil law are applied to the facts of the particular case. With the exception of minors and those declared incompetent, almost any member of society can be sued, that is, can be called to answer to society's code of behavior. A most central tenet of this code is the deterrence of recklessness.

If you are like most practitioners, facing a lawsuit would put you to a test for which you have not been prepared. Facing a lawsuit is a unique and stressful experience that is often equated to a crisis. For one thing, you may face a situation you have never experienced before: In a lawsuit, you cannot expect that your personal clinical judgment will prevail. The rules for the legal contest are already established, and your attorney will probably frame your testimony according to legal principles chosen for tactical reasons. These legal principles may or may not seem compatible with your clinical judgment. In addition, you must assume that whatever clinical and professional evidence you provide will be countered, even contradicted, by a psychologist colleague (or another professional deemed qualified) testifying for the plaintiff. The outcome of this contest may eventually turn on strictly clinical matters, but it is likely that this will happen only after the argument is framed within the rules of accepted legal procedure. More frequently, the outcome is determined by legal issues.

Duty of Care

Innocent people often get hurt when a certain duty of care is not maintained; this is the underlying principle of malpractice litigation and court decisions in malpractice cases. Different courts use different words to define and describe this duty, but typically it is defined as the care an ordinary, average person should exercise under such circumstances. All psychologists are required to fulfill this duty in both their personal and professional lives. Should they fail to do so, their act or failure to act is called *negligence*. If this negligence appears to lead to someone's being harmed, then that person could have grounds for a successful lawsuit.

Psychologists (and other licensed or certified mental health providers), like other members of society, owe a duty to society. However, they are also included in a higher category—professionals—who must act under the terms of a more demanding social contract. Together with physicians, lawyers, and many others, practitioners delivering psychological services owe a duty of care that is defined differently. For practitioners who offer their skills as professionals to the public, the legal test for negligence compares their performance with that of their professional peers. Thus, the standards under which they must work require that they go beyond simple caution.

Negligence, Malpractice, and Duty of Care: Key Concepts

• Most malpractice cases turn on the question of negligence. The plaintiff must prove that the defendant's actions failed to meet the relevant standard of care. The court usually requires that evidence be given that will specify exactly what the defendant's duty was. This is done by comparing the practitioner's performance with that of other professionals in the same community with comparable training and experience, even if the duty performed did not require that degree of professionalism. Typically, most of the evidence on this question will involve a debate over the clinical correctness and efficacy of the treatment that was given, along with the defendant's judgment in choosing it.

• A successful lawsuit, however, usually requires more to be proven than that the defendant was negligent in regard to the treatment. If the plaintiff fails to prove that real harm was suffered, the defendant will prevail. If the claim is for strictly mental and emotional harm, the practitioner being sued is more likely to be exonerated than if palpable physical injury or loss of something tangible can be proven.

- One important area of contention in most malpractice cases is the question of cause. The law puts a heavy burden on the plaintiff to prove that the defendant's negligent act was the primary and direct cause of the harm. The tests for this proof are very strict, and not infrequently the defendant will be exonerated because an additional event beyond his or her control contributed to the harm.

- In most cases involving issues of clinical malpractice, the client is expected to have met a standard of self-care; that is, the client is expected to have cooperated in treatment. The failure to have done so may often result in a case being dismissed or being denied because of the plaintiff's own negligence.

- Of the cases that proceed to trial, more practitioners probably win than lose a lawsuit because the plaintiff must meet some very strict legal tests. However, juries and even judges will depart on occasion from the strict guidelines that have been established, and their prerogative to do so may be vindicated on appeal.

- A final factor that is difficult to evaluate involves cost—the emotional costs, the drain on time and other resources, and the possible damage to one's reputation, even when the lawsuit is defeated in court. Vindication alone may not compensate the practitioner for such losses.

The Legal Definition of Malpractice

Virtually all legal disputes revolve around the idea of *rights and obligations*. When a practitioner undertakes to treat, diagnose, assess, or in any way advise or provide psychological services to a client, that practitioner is obliged to exercise a certain standard of care and service delivery. For the practitioner to be found negligent, it must be shown that he or she did not exercise the standard and, by failing to do so, injured the client (the plaintiff in the suit). Only when this is proven can the practitioner be held liable for monetary damages. Most other professional liability stems from a complainant's right to various guarantees under the law, such as the right to privacy, treatment, freedom from false imprisonment, and other special (psychology-related) legal interpretations of the general rules of law (mutual rights and obligations) that comprise the social contract in America.

Malpractice as a legal term describes all complaints in which a professional is accused of negligence in the context of a professional relationship. This is the meaning most often employed by those who write laws and by those who write about the law. Others include in the category of malpractice a wider catalog of legal problems faced by mental health providers. Practitioners can be sued for breach of contract and can also be accused of breaching one or more of a client's specific rights. However, the legal system discriminates between these kinds of disputes.

The law of malpractice proper refers to *unintentional* torts. A *tort* is a wrong that violates the civil code of society. The word *unintentional* does not necessarily mean that a person did wrong by accident but rather that the person *should have been aware* of certain duties to the other person. A law may or may not have been broken that would put the defendant in criminal jeopardy. Regardless, any action "in tort" is between individuals, each of whom will hire a lawyer. The plaintiff files a civil lawsuit for monetary damages at the appropriate court office. In criminal cases, the defendant is legally entitled to be defended, and if he or she cannot afford a lawyer, the court must provide one. In civil cases like a malpractice lawsuit, however, the defendant is not entitled to a legal defense and must hire a lawyer if he or she wants one. In practice, this legal defense is the first and most essential component of professional liability insurance (PLI).

Only mental health practitioners designated as *professionals* by law can be sued for malpractice. The mental health providers who are so designated will vary from state to state. In most states, the litmus test for *professional malpractice* (but not for other alleged actions) is that a practitioner be licensed or certified. Some states may also admit evidence about certification and even about education and training. Mental health professionals who fall outside these criteria, if sued, will most likely be judged by different standards. Anyone can be accused of, and found liable for, negligence. But professional negligence is measured against a higher standard.

The Four Elements of Malpractice

To succeed in a malpractice claim, the plaintiff must prove a case that stands on the following four distinct legs, called *elements of malpractice*:

1. A *professional relationship* was formed between the psychologist and client. Only thus does a practitioner incur a legal duty of care.
2. There is a *demonstrable* standard of care, and the practitioner breached that standard. He or she is said to have practiced "below the standard of care."
3. The client suffered *harm or injury*, which must be demonstrated and established.
4. The practitioner's breach of duty to practice within the standard of care was the *proximate cause* of the client's injury; that is, the injury was a reasonably foreseeable consequence of the breach.

The plaintiff bears the burden of proving the existence of each element for successful malpractice litigation. If more than one cause of action is cited, the plaintiff is required to prove each of the four elements for each of the torts. In practice, juries sometimes find a defendant negligent even though the proof for an element of the case is questionable. The jury system is not infallible, however, and such cases might be overturned on appeal.[1]

The Professional Relationship: When Do You Owe a Duty of Care?

As noted above, the plaintiff must prove that the practitioner undertook to provide services to the client. A formal contract between the parties is not necessary to prove this. For example, if the practitioner rendered a bill, the relationship is legally established. The legal theory used to support the establishment of duty derives from the theory of contracts, wherein a number of implicit acts will establish the connection. In the areas of medicine and therapy, however, attorneys also have recourse

---

[1]Most PLI policies, however, do not compel the carrier to appeal a loss. As an individual, one would probably be entitled to do so but would have to do so at one's own expense.

to the *undertaking* theory, which relies on evidence that actions taken constitute an intent to render service. Whether payment was demanded or made is not necessarily a consideration in determining whether a professional relationship was formal.

Clients in any ward or clinic, whether voluntarily or involuntarily admitted, will generally be able to establish the duty owed by almost anyone who ministers to them under the dominion of the institution. Entries by the professional in a chart or a professional's work-up notes usually provide sufficient evidence. Providing treatment in an emergency room or similar setting also carries this implication, as the client might reasonably conclude that because dispensing help is the business of such an operation, it will be done by professionals according to the relevant standard of care. But when a practitioner becomes involved in an emergency that arises outside of such an institution, especially an emergency involving someone not previously identified as a client, the question of whether the duty of care was assumed or undertaken might be hotly contested.

Psychologists, particularly those in private practice, rely on reputation, referrals, and word of mouth to find most of their clients. If a phone call or, more rarely, an emergency visit (possibly unannounced) was your first contact with someone, the law would probably look to the way you conducted yourself to determine whether you implicitly assumed a duty of care. If the person knew, or had cause to suspect, that you were a psychologist, then it would be your burden to prove that you explicitly and consistently warned that person that you were not becoming involved in your professional capacity. And even if you succeed in proving that you verbally denied the duty, it is conceivable that your actions will be interpreted as having spoken for themselves.

One dilemma is faced routinely by nearly all psychologists who, like physicians, are apt to be "consulted" by friends and even casual acquaintances with the proverbial "curious problem you might be interested in." If the inquiry comes from a friend, you may wish to consider a proper referral to another practitioner. If the inquiry comes from a casual acquaintance or another individual who will not present a conflict of interest problem, you should suggest that he or she call you to set up an appointment. This should clearly indicate that the relationship will be professional in nature.

Common sense would suggest that people who solicit such "opinions," as well as those who try to get "therapy" from publications, radio, or television, are on notice that the practitioner is not their therapist. However, neither the people who seek help in such ways nor the courts necessarily rely on common sense. Therefore caveats and disclaimers are always in order, as is attention to the relevant APA guidelines.

Some practitioners prefer to write treatment contracts with their clients. To the extent that the *therapeutic contract* is explicit, you might find yourself sued not for negligence per se but for breach of contract. This type of action does not fall under unintentional torts, the subject of this section. As such, the legal battle will ensue in a different context, one in which negligence often need not be proven. If you routinely or occasionally write an explicit contract with your clients, you need to be aware of the specific legal implications for a subsequent lawsuit (see pp. 51, 54, 97).

The psychotherapy relationship is inherently complex, no matter what your school or orientation. Nevertheless, during the initial sessions of treatment, many practitioners attempt to establish therapy goals to help foster an atmosphere of mutual accountability and responsibility. The intent is usually to establish a psychological atmosphere (as opposed to a legal contract) conducive to a certain tone and style of therapy. In most instances, clients share such concerns. Nonetheless, be aware that your client may view the act of establishing explicit goals as an implied promise of successful treatment. Therefore you might be providing the client with a stronger basis for legal action in the form of an explicit promise.

The Standard of Care: What Is Appropriate Treatment?

The medical profession was among the first professions to be held accountable for the delivery of care under the law. As a result, there is a large body of common law that refers to medical malpractice. The standards, concepts, and language that have developed in that tradition are cited frequently as being relevant to malpractice cases in which psychological negligence is alleged. For example, as we discussed previously, the appearance of caring for a client may lead to the legal conclusion that a practitioner undertook a duty of care. This concept has a long history in the common law surrounding the practice of medicine and has been successfully expanded to include the delivery of mental health services. Another dictum from the history of medical litigation is that the services rendered must be demonstrated to have been "at least as competently and skillfully performed as by the ordinary practitioner."

As previously noted, the legal concept of negligence is based on the premise that all members of society owe to one another the duty to exercise a certain inherent standard of care. In most malpractice claims, the plaintiff is required to prove that the defendant practitioner failed in his or her duty (that is, was negligent in upholding the relevant standard of care). Once it has been proven that a professional relationship was formed (the first of the four elements that must be proven) then *a duty owed* is established. Two questions must then be answered: (a) How is that duty defined? and (b) Has the practitioner fulfilled that duty? Perhaps as many as two out of every three suits brought against mental health providers will turn on these central questions.

A negligence case between ordinary citizens usually revolves around the test of what would be "customary for a reasonable, average person to do" when faced with the circumstances of the case. The same concept applies when the defendant's status as a professional turns the matter into a malpractice claim, but the standard for professionals is elevated because of the professional's presumptive training and abilities.

In most cases, the courts will look to the profession itself to define which standard should be used. In the courtroom, attorneys will develop evidence to define the *customary* standard applied by others in the field, with *field* defined in the most specific sense possible. For example, when a clinical psychologist who has been trained in cognitive techniques (and offers this orientation explicitly to his or her clients) comes to the courtroom, the standard for his or her professional performance is predefined. The cognitive school is recognized by the community of psychologists as a distinct and viable orientation, with well-defined standards for training and clinical guidelines. The attorneys must present evidence confined to the practice of clinical psychology, with reference to the defendant's experience, self-advertisement, and theoretical orientation. Such evidence usually is presented in the form of expert testimony from others with a similar profile and may, on occasion, include published standards, codes, and guidelines.

In both medical and psychological malpractice, the courts used to look into the local community to find a hypothetical "ordinary, average" practitioner against whom to measure the defendant. This *locality rule* reflected a two-fold concern. First, it was believed that the comparative isolation and rudimentary conditions faced by certain rural practitioners might inhibit them from developing sophisticated skills such as those of their colleagues in large cities and major medical centers. Second, its roots reflected feeling that local professionals knew best the indigenous peculiarities and needs of their neighbors. Generally speaking, this test of locality has been relegated to the dustbin as modern technology and more accessible cables of communication have continued to knit Americans together in a common, national experience. However, the consensus about whether locality is an issue is not without exception. Rulings in any particular region or state may still be carving out "local" standards.

When the locality rule reigned, however, observers of the system were heard to decry a "conspiracy of silence." Because comparable practitioners from the same community were likely to have professional and personal relations with the defendant, it was believed that they might bring to the courtroom an understandable reluctance to deliver what could be damaging testimony against their colleague or friend. Critics observed elements of self-interest, retaliation, and collegial "circling of the wagons" that compromised the accuracy and completeness of the evidentiary search for the standard of care. When the obligation to find the expert from the same community was relieved, the problem of finding practitioners willing to testify also disappeared. Magazines and journals for trial lawyers now routinely include advertisements by people eager to travel and provide their professional opinions for a fee. However, such "hired guns" are generally not viewed favorably by members of the profession.

Case law on the standard of care question varies around the country. Some courts will put the emphasis on *accepted* practice, others on what is *customary*. Psychologists who develop or subscribe to innovative therapies might find themselves having to prove that a "respectable minority" of their profession concurs in their techniques or treatment strategies. It is not unknown, however, for a court to develop a consensus from expert witnesses about a standard and then to find it inadequate. Such judicial criticism of an entire profession is rare but serves to illustrate that the rules of procedure are not ironclad.

Alternatively, the standard of care can derive not from one's own training but from the clinical imperatives of the client's condition. The general rule that one will be held to the same standard as others with the same training and orientation does not necessarily hold if the client's condition dictates that one should have referred the client to someone with greater or different expertise. For example, if evidence about the presenting symptoms suggests that a medical opinion should have been obtained, the court may impose standards related to the necessity for medical referral. If the practitioner is not qualified or trained to deliver certain services, then he or she has an *obligation* to properly diagnose and refer.

Another exception to the strict application of the doctrine occurs when a "lower" level of expertise is normally appropriate. If you have been trained and certified as a clinical psychologist, you can be held to that standard even if the role you were fulfilling at the time did not require a clinician of that degree.

Many sets of guidelines, even codes of ethics such as the APA *Ethical Principles*, have been incorporated into laws that govern the licensure and regulation of psychologists. Often such material is introduced as evidence of the standard of care that should be applied to a particular case. In rare cases, expert testimony might even be obviated if the court can look directly to a statute to establish the standard.

Given the adversarial nature of the lawsuit, a defendant psychologist might even expect the plaintiff's attorney to argue against applying a particular standard if the attorney expects it to vindicate the correctness of the defendant's behavior. On occasion, plaintiffs will argue that expert testimony is not needed because the act in question is negligence per se and thus violates a more basic standard of common sense. If this is permitted, the jury must decide the matter of negligence without reliance on expert testimony.

Similarly, the plaintiff may try to invoke the legal principle of *res ipsa loquitur*. Common to these sorts of cases is a situation in which only the defendant and not the plaintiff has direct knowledge of what happened. For example, if an eclectic therapist not fully certified in the practice of hypnosis used an hypnotic procedure that involved a regression and obtained primitive material in relation to the hypnotic episode, but unintended negative clinical consequences resulted, then the plaintiff's attorney might use this principle. Moreover, it must be demonstrated that harm rarely occurs in that "generic" factual situation unless there is negligence. If the court accepts this premise, then an altogether different set of presumptions is invoked. Expert testimony may be obviated altogether or may be limited to statement that "harm rarely occurs in similar situations without negligence." The defendant must contend with the inference that the plaintiff's injury would not have occurred if not for the negligent act of the defendant. However, plaintiffs in such cases

- must also be innocent of contributing to the injury,
- must show that the defendant had exclusive control over whatever caused the injury, and
- must prove that if the defendant had managed it properly, the injury would not have occurred.

A plaintiff may be motivated to invoke *res ipsa loquitur* because, in many situations, these tests are easier to prove than the standard four elements of a malpractice case.

Proving Injuries: Was There Harm Done?

Recall that proving malpractice requires that all four elements of proof be met. Whether a duty is owed (element 1) is often clear; whether the standard of care in fulfilling that duty has been upheld (element 2) often goes to the heart of the accusation of negligence. The third element of malpractice—Was harm done?—is more easily defined than proven. Three kinds of harm, injury, or damage may be claimed by the plaintiff:

1. An indisputable physical injury or death has either befallen or been inflicted by the client. If such damage is present, the emphasis will shift to proving that the practitioner's actions comprised proximate and legal cause.
2. The injury cited (e.g., loss of wages or other economic harm, divorce) is consequent to the act in question. The plaintiff must show that these injuries were the results of behavior "directed or caused" by the therapist.
3. The injury claimed may be largely subjective, that is to say, the harm may consist primarily of mental effects in the client, commonly referred to as *pain and suffering*.

The first two classes of injuries speak for themselves. The third type, pain and suffering, deserves some elaboration. Courts historically have been reluctant to award monetary damages for emotional injuries. As a rule, only in the most dramatic cases have juries recompensed claimants for pain and suffering. However, in recent years, the increase in knowledge about the psyche has substantiated a much wider catalog of potential mental injury. With particular reference to psychotherapy clients, the following effects (Strupp, Hadley, & Gormes-Schwartz, 1977, as cited in Schutz, 1982) could be bases for liability if proven to occur as the result of a practitioner's action (or inaction):

• Exacerbation of the presenting symptoms (including decompensation or regression, increased depression, inhibitions, extension of phobias, increased somatic difficulties, decreased self-esteem, paranoia, obsessional symptoms, guilt, decrease in impulse control)

• Appearance of new symptoms (including psychotic break or dissociations, severe psychosomatic reactions, suicide attempt, development of new forms of acting out, disruption of previously solid relationships)

• Client misuse or abuse of therapy (generally settling into a dependent relationship that is more gratifying than the "real" world, increase in intellectualization to avoid action or as a mere change of obsessional thoughts, use of therapy as a place to merely ventilate hostile feelings and have them rationalized, increased reliance on irrationality and "spontaneity" to avoid reflection on real-world limits)

• Clients overextending themselves in taking on tasks before they can adequately achieve them, possibly to please the therapist or due to inappropriate directives, leading to failure, guilt, or self-contempt

• Disillusionment with therapy, leading to feelings of hopelessness in getting help from any relationship.[2]

This is a rather daunting list of psychological and behavioral sequelae that covers almost every possibility. However, to hypothesize or even to prove that such effects have occurred is by no means enough. To sustain a complaint for negligence, the plaintiff must demonstrate what usually turns out to be the most difficult of

---

[2]Adapted from Schutz (1982, pp. 8–9) by permission.

connections, that the therapist's negligent act *caused* the injury. And on this point of causation the law is quite explicit.

Proving Cause: Did The Practitioner Contribute?

Notice that the word *cause* in the legal context is usually preceded by two modifiers, *legal* and *proximate*. Legal cause may also be referred to as a cause in fact. The test of legal cause is usually that the harm would not have occurred but for the alleged act, which also can be an omission or failure to act. Proximate cause adds two other tests: The alleged act must have been (a) the direct and reasonably foreseeable cause and (b) the primary cause of the harm. The burden is on the plaintiff to prove that the psychologist's negligent act was both the proximate and the legal cause of the loss or injury. This is not an easy task.

Defense Against Injuries and Proximate Cause

Chain of Events

To prevail in litigation, the plaintiff must demonstrate that a natural and unbroken sequence of events occurred and resulted in the injury and, furthermore, that all of these events were the responsibility of the defendant alone. This has been called the *chain of events*, which must remain unbroken if the defendant is to be properly adjudged negligent. Any intervening events that disrupt the chain, unless they were caused by an earlier act of the defendant and could have been reasonably foreseen, will tend to break the chain and may absolve the defendant.

This chain of events requirement can lead to a finding of no negligence because of superseding, intervening events (no proximate cause). It can also lead to a defense commonly used in negligence lawsuits—*contributory negligence* by the plaintiff. As a citizen and member of society, the plaintiff has a duty to maintain a certain standard of self-care. If the plaintiff fails in this duty, that failure could lead to an act that in whole or in part led to the harm suffered by the plaintiff. Thus, the defendant could be totally or partially absolved of responsibility if his or her acts, even though proven to have caused the harm, were not the sole cause.[3]

Statute of Limitations

Another defense to malpractice charges involves the statute of limitations (discussed in detail on pp. 106–107), which restricts to a specified period the time allowed for a complaint to be filed after an injury has occurred. Connecting the alleged act and its consequent harm may be inherently problematic. Thus, the law discourages frivolous or belated suits in which the evidence developed to support the claim comes too late after the facts that gave rise to the claim. While the statute of limitations for many medical and psychological claims is often shorter than for

---

[3]This doctrine is not applied to minors or to those legally declared incompetent, to whom a practitioner has an even greater professional responsibility.

negligence suits directed against nonprofessionals, there are a number of variations and technicalities involved.

The time limit (statute of limitations) for filing a suit varies from state to state and may differ depending on the nature of the complaint. It may date not from the alleged negligence but from *discovery* of the injury. Also, only those judged to be competent adults may sue. Thus, a client who may have been incompetent at the time the alleged injury occurred and who later regains competence would have from the time of regaining competence to the end of the statute of limitations to file a claim, even though the event may have occurred years or decades before. And the clock on actions brought by or on behalf of minors does not begin ticking until they come of age. Finally, the time allowed for filing does not start with the first act of negligence. If the behavior that led to the complaint continued over a course of time, which is frequently the case in psychological treatment, the statute begins to run only when the negligent act has ceased.

An Imperfect System

One final comment to this modest examination or overview of malpractice law: The practitioner cannot expect something as complex as a lawsuit, involving so many questions of judgment, to be run like a close-order drill. In fact, the jury system may be said to infuse the proceedings with additional human error, in the sense that juries (and at times even judges) depart from the letter of the law to administer justice as they see it.

The procedural rules of malpractice law are explicit, but if they are not upheld, one may not automatically have a successful means of correction or appeal. And the rules are in flux. For example, recent court rulings in areas not far distant from psychological malpractice have begun to invoke the principle of *strict liability*. Simply put, under this doctrine, the concept of negligence is removed altogether from a lawsuit. If a demonstrable harm has been done, the practitioner could be held liable just for performing the act that led to it, even if every conceivable precaution was taken and the harm could not easily be foreseen. This is clearly a social rather than a judicial phenomenon, but the courts, in the final analysis, are a mediation ground. They try to bring the law and the people together. As times change, so too does the law.

Part II ————————————————

Being Prepared
Day-to-Day

4

What This Section Is Designed To Do: Individual Focus Lists

As already noted, most concerns involving ethics and potential liability stem from a surprisingly small number of issues (listed here in the order of frequency with which liability suits are brought): sexual improprieties, other dual relationships, fee collection, undue influence, breach of contract, abandonment, failure to cure (and poor results), failure to refer, and failure to treat. Underlying most of these issues are questions related to what constitutes the therapeutic contract and informed consent.

No matter how prescriptive and definitive the methods and principles of a particular school of therapy or technique may be, no matter how ethical or skilled in business procedures a psychologist may be, there is always a potential for error or misunderstanding. Each psychologist forms unique relationships with individual clients, the community, local and state bureaucracies, and other elements of the environment in which the professional works and lives. Regardless of the relationship, complications most often arise not from foreseeable problems but rather from a psychologist's failure to anticipate and recognize potential problem areas. It is incumbent upon the practitioner to develop an awareness of—and to guard against—self-defeating behaviors and behaviors that may harm the client and the profession. It is important to maintain a distinct clinical perspective on the practical, day-to-day aspects of one's actions.

The focus lists that follow were compiled to:

- remind you of some of your ethical and legal obligations
- elevate your awareness regarding questions to ask
- suggest possible risk management procedures you can generally incorporate into practice with relative ease.

Each item in the focus lists has been selected because it may be useful in improving practice and in helping you avoid malpractice pitfalls. *These items are not intended to establish standards of practice.* Nor are all possible issues, events, or procedures touched upon. The focus lists are not intended to say, "Practice defensively" or "You are wrong if you practice any other way but this." Nor are they intended to say, "Do this and you will never have a problem." They are intended to convey the message, "You can practice in a way that is professional and that protects you and your clients. You can practice wisely and well."

The Structure of the Focus Lists

There are 31 focus lists. Each covers an area of specific concern, such as terminating a therapeutic relationship. Some lists stand alone, that is, they can be used without other lists. If there are other focus lists to which you should refer, they are cited by focus list number in the text.

The focus lists fall roughly into four groups:

- Lists 1–9 cover overarching issues such as basic tools of the professional practitioner and dual relationships.
- Lists 10–16 discuss specific treatment concerns such as testing and dangerousness.
- Lists 17–29 cover operational concerns such as record keeping and preparing for retirement.
- Lists 30 and 31 cover handling complaints and being sued.

Focus 1: The Basic Tools of the Professional Psychologist

- Do you know and understand the ethics and practice guidelines of the profession? Do you review them periodically and use them as a decision-making tool?
- Are you conversant with local and state laws that govern your practice, especially as they relate to the topics discussed in this volume? It is impossible to memorize every law and every case application of a law, but do you strive to gain an understanding of strictures placed on practice and of how those laws are being interpreted in particular cases, especially those in which consumer rights are at issue?
- Do you uphold and foster the highest practice guidelines? Do you support the effort to improve guidelines that exist and enforce their application?
- Do you tolerate violations of ethics and practice guidelines by a colleague? (See chapter 2, p. 26.)
- Do you acknowledge your own vulnerability to error and misinterpretation? Do you consider your actions in relation to ethics and practice guidelines?
- Are you flexible and open to change? Do you anticipate new demands and new knowledge as well as the need for a fresh outlook that new clients and situations may demand?
- Do you make a conscious effort to evaluate your own actions and improve the ways in which you work, communicate, and foster professional relationships with others?

Focus 2: Competency as a Professional

- Do you know the specific licensing requirements in your state, including required credentials and renewal periods, that govern your practice? Do you review these periodically and allow adequate time to comply with them?
- Are you thoroughly familiar with differences and potential conflicts between the state's requirements and the ethics, standards, and principles defining compe-

tency within the profession? Do you perform according to the highest requirements for quality and service?

- Do you take steps (e.g., pursuing continuing education) to maintain your competency, even if none are required by the state laws?

- Do you support the maintenance and enhancement of practice guidelines and ethics within the profession and expect your colleagues to uphold existing guidelines?

Active Self-Awareness

- Do you periodically evaluate your own skills and qualifications to provide the services you have traditionally provided?

- If a client, colleague, or employee criticizes an aspect of your professional behavior, do you consider the critique carefully and objectively? If necessary, do you seek the advice of an experienced colleague?

- Do you exaggerate the nature or level of your skills and qualifications or claim those that you do not possess?

- Do you acquire the skills and knowledge necessary to provide a service before attempting to provide it without supervision?

- If you undertake continuing education, do you obtain it only from individuals or organizations who have been certified or licensed, or both, by an appropriate agency (e.g., the American Psychological Association [APA] Continuing Education Program or a state agency)?

- Are you alert to signs of fatigue and burnout in yourself?

- Are you alert to signs that the therapy is not working, and do you take steps to put things back on track? It may be useful to consult a colleague.

- If your efforts do not improve the results, or further deterioration occurs, do you seek consultation or consider terminating the therapy and referring the client to a colleague for treatment?

- In areas where there is little or no established procedure, do you discuss treatment options and implications with experienced colleagues? If appropriate, do you alert clients to your use of a technique with which you have limited familiarity and provide safeguards for the client?

Supervising Others

- Have you learned the skills necessary to supervise, whether those skills relate to teaching and training students or to overseeing the work of an employee?

- If you teach students, supervise interns, or direct other training programs, do you provide those you teach with appropriate and timely support and guidance and a firm grounding in the knowledge, skills, and ethics required to provide their future clients with appropriate care?

- Do you instruct those you supervise to adhere to the tenets of the profession that are relevant to them and to perform tasks that they are qualified and legally and ethically certified or licensed to perform?

- Have you established procedures for providing evaluations of employees or students in a timely manner? Have you included provisions for both oral and written evaluations? Do you document even oral evaluations?
- Do you provide accurate references? If you are concerned about a person's reactions to a poor reference, do you consider alternatives such as only confirming dates of employment or study, only providing grades and indicating that the individual needed improvement in a given area, or, if feasible, giving no reference? When you are in doubt, do you consult a more experienced colleague?
- Do you maintain accurate documentation of performance, including positive and negative aspects, written evaluations, factual observations, work history, reasons for termination, and similar information? Do you include records of references provided?

Focus 3: Consent to Treatment

- All clients, regardless of their capacity to understand, have the right to have treatment explained to them. In most cases, informed consent requires the client to be competent, to have knowledge of what will occur, and to be willing to be treated. The exceptions include court-ordered evaluation or treatment, absence of competence, and similar circumstances that may vary from state to state.
- A competent client who is not under legal compulsion (e.g., court-ordered evaluation or treatment) has the right to withdraw consent at any time, for any reason. This must be explained to the client.
- Share information within the capacity of the client to understand and as it is appropriate for the treatment being provided. Do not withhold material information from the client.
- Do you avoid using jargon when discussing treatment with a client? Do you use language appropriate for the client's understanding?
- If the individual has a hearing impairment or there is a language barrier, do you obtain the assistance of a signer or translator?
- Do you plan carefully for how you will explain the treatment to the client, especially if he or she is a child or will have difficulty understanding treatment because of illness or mental incapacity?
- If there are other special circumstances with which you have limited experience (e.g., cultural barriers), do you consult a colleague experienced in treating such patients and, if necessary, refer the client?
- Do you avoid making assumptions about the client's ability to understand?

Obtaining Informed Consent

- If you have doubts about the client's competence, do you evaluate the client?
- If possible, before treatment begins, do you adequately inform clients and their parents or guardians, as appropriate, about treatment?
- If circumstances prevent you from informing the client or his or her parent or guardian before treatment begins, do you take the earliest opportunity to do so?

- Do you describe the treatment approach and its risks and benefits, as well as possible alternatives (including no treatment) and their risks and benefits, in sufficient detail to ensure that the client understands the procedures?
- Do you use an educative approach by inviting questions, testing the client's understanding, and providing appropriate feedback (and reinforcement as treatment proceeds)?
- If you use written consent forms, do you have the client or client's parent or guardian sign the form before treatment begins, if at all possible, or as soon as possible thereafter?

Documentation

- Do you record the nature of the consent, either by having the client (or parent or guardian) sign a written consent form (see below for the possible content of such a form) or by including in the client's file a detailed, written report of what you told the client (or parent or guardian) about the therapy and other matters relevant to consent?
- Do you note in the client's file any matters that affect informed consent, such as the client's degree of emotional upset?
- Do you indicate circumstances that altered how you obtained consent or why you failed to obtain it prior to treatment? These circumstances could include emergencies (e.g., threatened suicide, violence, extreme physical duress), incompetence, court-ordered evaluation or treatment, or the degree of influence that was needed to bring the client to treatment (and who influenced him or her).
- Do you provide the client (or parent or guardian) with a copy of the signed consent form?
- A written consent form could include:
  1. date of discussion regarding consent
  2. your name and the patient's name, preferably typed
  3. a sentence affirming that the client understood what he or she was told
  4. a statement of the client's right to withdraw consent
  5. a description of the kind of treatment to be provided (this may be particularly relevant if experimental treatment is being offered)
  6. a signature of the client or parent or guardian.
- If you feel it to be necessary, you could consult an attorney regarding the content of such a form.
- Consent to treatment can be part of a written treatment contract.

Focus 4: Evaluating the Competency of a Client

- In some states or settings, psychologists' roles in evaluating and determining competence are very limited. Regardless, psychologists do perform evaluations on behalf of other professionals and should understand the requirements of such evaluations.

- Unless legally adjudged to be incompetent, all adults are presumed to be competent. Overruling the right of a client to self-determination is the function of the courts.
- Are you familiar with conditions that present special concern about competency to receive treatment, such as extreme psychosis, depression, suicidal impulse, and Alzheimer's disease, so that you at least know the superficial indicators of competency and the reasons for concern regarding the patient's welfare?
- Do you refer clients whose conditions are obviously not within your competence to evaluate (e.g., if you have no experience with suicidal or violent patients, do you consider referring them to a more experienced colleague)?
- In emergency situations, if possible, thoroughly evaluate the client prior to initiating treatment, but do not withhold clearly indicated treatment in the absence of evaluation. Evaluate the client as soon as possible.
- Do you consult with appropriate specialists (e.g., physicians, individuals experienced in working with alcoholics) regarding the special conditions the client presents?
- Do you consult with therapists or others who treated the client previously, if permitted by the client? If the client refuses such permission, do you document the refusal in the client's record?
- Do you consult with family members, co-workers, friends, or others, if appropriate, obtaining as much relevant information as possible?
- Before consulting with others, do you obtain consent for the release of information from the client? Some state statutes permit such consultation without the consent of the client in emergency situations. Do you keep abreast of state laws concerning issues of privilege and confidentiality?
- Do you consider the following when evaluating the client?
  1. age, sex, and relevant ethnic and cultural factors
  2. physical condition of the client
  3. history (of both the client and his or her family)
  4. history of substance abuse
  5. medical history, including prescription drug use
  6. degree of awareness and orientation
  7. degree of function required of the client
  8. degree of your understanding of the facts of the case
  9. the client's degree of stress associated with the reason treatment is being sought
  10. the circumstances under which he or she came to treatment
  11. the lack of familiarity with you and the therapeutic relationship
  12. the degree and nature of influence used, if any, by others to bring the client into therapy
  13. the prognosis for the client's presenting condition in relation to continued competence without care
- Do you try to interview the client more than once?
- Are you careful in using evaluative measures and tests? Do you explain the purpose and result of testing to the client (or parent or guardian) as appropriate?
- If the evaluation reveals that the client is not competent to consent to treatment (or not competent to function without guardianship) and he or she is without

a legal guardian, do you aid in identifying a guardian for that client? Consider the following:

1. Is there a relative who is willing and appropriate to serve in that capacity?
2. If not, is there a friend, attorney, member of the clergy, or other individual who could serve?
3. If not, are there legal agencies that could serve?
4. The criteria should include willingness, lack of conflict of interest, understanding of the client's condition, and similar issues reflecting the need to support the client's maintenance and improvement.

Focus 5: The Therapeutic Contract

• You have ethical and legal responsibilities to protect a potential client's welfare, beginning even from the first professional contact with that client.

• All clients are entitled to treatment, regardless of the problem they present, their capacity to pay, whether or not they are difficult to work with, or the difficulty of treating the disorder. If you are able and qualified, you may be ethically responsible to provide that treatment. You should assist the clients in finding treatment regardless of such circumstances.

• Even though the terms of services that you are to provide are described in a contract, your legal obligations may go beyond what is written down. Contracts can include implied responsibility and acknowledged (but unwritten) understandings of what constitutes accepted therapeutic or professional practice.

• Contracts may be both written and oral. What you tell a client and document in your records may be construed as part of an implied contract.

• Do you avoid making oral and written promises of cure?

• Do you accurately state your policies and practices when speaking with a client?

Questions To Ask Before Accepting a Client

• Is the form of therapy you offer appropriate for this client? Do you consider the nature of the therapy, what the goals are, and the viewpoint of the client? Do you consider the client's belief systems in relation to the goals and techniques of the therapy?

• Do you use persuasive techniques carefully and minimize client risk? Subtle pressure may be appropriate, but coercion is not. (See Focus 12.)

• Do you consider whether you can work with this client? Does he or she have personality traits that would make it impossible for you to treat him or her effectively?

• Do you consider whether the client has special needs and whether you can adapt to them? For example,

1. Is there a physical challenge present (e.g., impairment of hearing or vision)?

2. If you speak only English, is the client also fluent in English?
3. If you speak the client's language, do you have the fluency necessary to provide therapy in that language?
4. Is a qualified person (signer, translator) available to help you overcome the communication gap?

• Do you ask whether the individual's special difference presents a challenge to your willingness to provide clinical services? Will you be able to adjust to those concerns and provide appropriate treatment?

• If you do not feel comfortable providing treatment, do you explain this to the client in terms of competence to provide treatment, if you can do so without harming the client? If necessary, do you discuss how to handle this issue (both in terms of the client's needs and your own) with a qualified colleague?

• Do you consider whether your client is a minor or under legal guardianship?
1. Is the client legally competent to consent to treatment?
2. If not, have you obtained a consent to treatment from an appropriate person or agency?
3. Does obtaining consent from someone other than the client pose difficulties for the client (e.g., does the client agree to treatment and are problems going to arise in treatment or later if he or she does not)?

• If you use experimental techniques, do you explain them as such and provide appropriate guidelines for yourself, any assistants you have, and the client? Do you take measures to minimize the risk to clients? Are you alert for signs of potential harm throughout treatment?

Considering What To Tell a Client

• Do you consider whether it is therapeutically necessary and appropriate to withhold from the client information about the form and techniques used in the therapy?

• Are you sensitive to concerns related to the client's right to be informed about his or her evaluation or treatment?

• Although it is true that some therapeutic procedures or interventions would be useless if explained in advance to the client, do you consider whether it may be appropriate to inform the client that some information will be witheld and to obtain consent?

• Do you plan how you will explain the process and progress of therapy to the client (and, when appropriate, family members) in light of the client's education and history? Are you prepared to explain in nonpsychological terms what will happen and why, and to do so in a way that does not damage the client's perception of his or her capacity to understand?

Preparing the Client for Therapy

• As appropriate, do you explain the treatment thoroughly and obtain informed consent?

- Do you explain that, as therapy progresses, some of the goals and methods involved may be changed and other may be added? Do you discuss how this will be handled?

- It is good business practice and a courtesy to your clients, as well as ethically appropriate in some instances, to provide information in writing, such as office hours, needed telephone numbers, a statement of policy regarding payment of bills, and so forth.

Group, Couples, or Family Therapy

- Do you select group participants carefully, considering whether the individual client can adapt to group dynamics and obtain effective treatment?

- Do you consider whether the individual will need to continue individual therapy as well as participate in group therapy? Do you consider carefully whether and how the treatment mixture will work?

- Do you consider the dynamics between couple and family members carefully before deciding to provide joint therapy? Can the couple or the family work together to resolve problems? Can they learn to do so with proper guidance? What special efforts will be required?

- Do you explain the terms of participation to each participant before the group, couples or family therapy begins, identifying differences between individual goals and therapy involving more than one person?

- Do you discuss with all participants in couples or family therapy both the special benefits and the risks of the format, particularly in terms of how it can change relationships?

- If you are not going to head the group and the client considers you to be his or her therapist of choice, do you work with the client to reach a mutual agreement regarding the group treatment, its value, and the appropriate relationship with the group therapist?

- Do you discuss the issue of confidentiality and the effects that group discussion of individual problems and concerns may have on the right to privacy? Do you include discussion of the relation between group discussions and individual therapy sessions that might be carried on in conjunction with the group, couples or family sessions?

- Are you aware of state and federal laws and regulations that impact on the issues of confidentiality as applied to group, marital, couples, or family therapy?

- If you provide marital therapy, have you developed and do you follow specific procedures related to confidentiality? Be aware that if the couple decides to separate or divorce, one spouse may wish to use information revealed during treatment in legal proceedings related to the divorce, property settlement, or custody disputes.

- If a client participates in group sessions and has individual sessions, do you maintain separate files for the two kinds of sessions? Confidentiality of individual sessions is more likely to be protected (although exceptions have been made) if a separate file is maintained.

- Are you careful to avoid discussing what happens to one client as an individual in either group or individual sessions with another client who participates in the group sessions?

• Do you respect each participant's rights as an individual as well as the commitment made by everyone to participate and the rights that participation brings?

• When the clients gather for the first meeting of the group, do you discuss the terms of participation, the purposes of the group therapy, the kinds of sharing that will occur (include the concept of confidentiality if relevant), and so forth, and ensure that a mutual understanding exists between and among you and the clients?

• If you consider having group members sign an agreement, you may wish to use one that:

1. states that members will hold in confidence all matters discussed in the group
2. indicates the limit of legal protection of privilege within group therapy (in some jurisdictions, there are laws protecting confidentiality in group therapy)
3. provides for signatures of all group members.

• If the group is an educational group, are you sensitive to the need to clarify the purposes of the program carefully and to adhere to appropriate guidelines for such groups?

Written Contracts

• You should consider very carefully the laws in your state that govern contracting, particularly in terms of consumer rights. Discuss the advisability, content, and standardization of content with a lawyer if you think it necessary.

• Consider whether a standardized contract can be used appropriately in each instance. Tailor contracts as needed.

• As appropriate, a written contract could include:

1. your name and the name of the client
2. a schedule for the sessions
3. the date the sessions will begin
4. a statement of goals
5. a statement regarding the fact that there is no guarantee of success but that you will apply your skills in good faith
6. a description of techniques that will be used
7. an express consent to use an experimental technique, if contemplated
8. a description of any potential negative effects of that treatment
9. a statement regarding freedom to negotiate or renegotiate the terms at any time
10. the amount of fees and schedule for payment
11. a statement of your policy for payment for missed appointments
12. a consent-to-treatment statement regarding informed consent
13. in some instances, a statement regarding the confidentiality of records and the limitations of confidentiality
14. the signatures of the client (or his or her guardian) and the therapist

• Provide the client with a copy of the signed contract.

Focus 6: Interrupted Therapy

- Any absence, even one caused by your being in a session with another client, may appear to a client to be abandonment. You cannot wholly prevent this, but you can ameliorate it.
- You cannot control all aspects of your life. Emergencies do occur, and you must provide for your own well-being. Take vacations and attend to personal needs so that you can continue to provide effective care to your client.
- Do you train staff thoroughly in procedures to follow in emergencies and other absences?
- Do you check your messages frequently? A patient in crisis or who is experiencing a personal emergency of another kind may feel abandoned by you if you do not respond to his or her call within a reasonable time period.

Planning for Interruptions in Therapy

- Have you established and do you follow a procedure for dealing with interruptions and emergencies?
    1. In emergencies, do you arrange for another therapist to stand in for you? Note that you should obtain clients' written consent to provide information to your substitute. This might be done in the form of a general release covering emergencies.
    2. Are you careful to insure that your substitute is qualified, both in training and in awareness of your clients' special needs, to deliver the services your clients may require?
    3. Do you inform your clients about your method of handling emergencies as part of their orientation to treatment? It can be problematic to wait until an emergency occurs.
    4. It might be useful to remind clients of your policy from time to time.
    5. It also might be useful to explain that emergencies can occur in both of your lives and to discuss the provisions for emergencies that the client may experience (e.g., whom to call), emphasizing that both of you have a responsibility to be present and on time for sessions.
- Are you prepared to deal with a client's unhappiness, even when he or she knows and understands the policy about emergencies? It is sometimes helpful to explain why you were absent, if appropriate, and to apologize.

Planning for Vacations and Long-Term Absences

- Do you arrange for coverage by a colleague who is experienced in areas pertinent to the needs of your clients, and do you orient each therapist to the cases that he or she may be called upon to handle? It might be helpful to schedule a meeting on your return to discuss what may have occurred during your absence.
- Do you prepare your clients for your absence? Within reason, you can explain why you will be absent and for how long.
- Explain to clients the procedures that they should follow while you are gone.

- Under some circumstances (e.g., possible surgery, long-term illness, pregnancy), it may be necessary to take special care to prepare your clients. Some reasons for absence, however positive for you, can be a painful, upsetting experience for some clients, one that manifests itself either before your absence or after your return. For other clients, if your absence is the result of a positive life event, the experience can be uplifting and can even enhance the therapeutic process. (See Focus 28.)

- On your return, do you discuss with your substitute any contacts he or she had with your clients?

- Do you address relevant matters as necessary during your clients' next sessions?

- Are you prepared for clients' reactions? Regardless of the steps you take, some clients will still feel that you abandoned them. This issue can provide an opportunity for constructive discussions during therapy. However, in some instances, a client's trust of you may be permanently damaged, sometimes to the point where it is best to terminate the relationship.

Focus 7: Terminating a Therapeutic Relationship

- The right to terminate therapy is a shared right. Both the client and the therapist have the right to end the relationship.

- The therapist has an additional responsibility to try to ensure that the client who needs therapy has continued therapeutic support.

Questioning the Client's Decision To End Therapy

- Do you maintain a professional attitude? Do you avoid arguing with the client or treating his or her decision as an attack on your abilities as a professional?

- If the client is willing to do so, do you discuss the reasons for his or her choosing to end therapy?

- If it is advisable, do you encourage the client to continue therapy with you and attempt to resolve the conflicts that have arisen in the context of the therapy you provide?

- If the client remains firm about ending therapy, but you feel that continuing therapy is vital to the client's well-being, do you encourage the client to continue therapy? Do you document such recommendations in the client's record?

- Do you provide a referral, if appropriate? Consider sending a follow-up letter providing names of individuals for referral.

- In some circumstances, and if the client is willing for you to do so, it may be appropriate to arrange for an appointment for the client with a new therapist.

Noting the Limitations of Your Training

- If the client presents conditions that you do not feel competent to treat, do you provide a referral rather than begin treatment?

- If you have been treating a client and he or she begins to present a condition that you do not feel competent to treat, do you discuss the matter with an experienced colleague? If appropriate, do you refer that client to another therapist for evaluation or treatment?

Preparing Clients To End Therapy

- Even clients who look forward to ending therapy may experience anxiety about leaving therapy.
- As the client demonstrates greater and greater autonomy, do you begin to prepare for the end of therapy?
- When appropriate, do you discuss ending the therapy openly with the client and confront the issues that arise?
- Do you work to develop a mutual agreement between you and the client that describes the termination? Consider:
  1. how many sessions remain
  2. the goals for those sessions
  3. the nature of the formal follow-up that might be required
  4. plans for any techniques the client might use to enhance the continued benefits of the therapy
  5. whether you will be available for consultation after the formal termination of therapy.
- If follow-up is a part of the agreement, do you clarify how the client should initiate the follow-up contact?
- Do you make it clear that the client may contact you should the need arise? Do you encourage the client to contact a therapist, even if you are not available, if he or she feels the need?
- At an appropriate point, do you remind the client of any business matters that remain (e.g., the need to pay any remaining charges or policies related to the release of information from the client's records)?
- Do you document the reason for termination, the client's reactions, details of the agreement, requirements for follow-up (including the name of any colleague to whom you may have referred the client for follow-up), and other details surrounding termination?
- Do you consider it appropriate to send a letter to the client after the sessions have ended? The letter could confirm the termination agreement and provide support for the client's continued autonomy. However, if the client was overly dependent, great care should be taken in preparing the text of such a letter.

Helping Clients Who Are Ready but Reluctant To Terminate

- Think through how you will approach the topic of termination. Consider possible objections that the client may raise and how you will address those objections. Be prepared to deal with an emotional reaction. Deal with the reluctance therapeutically. Also, remember that some clients may even react with extreme aggressiveness or even violence.

- Use caution: Avoid terminating a client whose clinical condition indicates the need for continued treatment.
- Use caution: If you work for a managed health care system that mandates termination at a specific time regardless of the client's condition, you should attempt to seek continuation of treatment or provide proper referral for additional treatment.
- Prolonged treatment may lead to dependence, which can result in the client's desiring to remain in treatment, even when it is time for the client to function on his or her own.
- Carefully select the time to discuss termination.
- Be open about the reasons for termination. Reassure the client that the termination is for his or her own well-being. Do not deceive the client regarding the reason for termination.
- If possible, behave toward and work with this client as you would a client who is agreeable to ending the relationship.
- Be prepared for the client to agree to terminate but to later take action against you on the grounds of abandonment.
- Do you record the details of termination carefully and fully? Send a letter to the client confirming the reasons for termination and reiterating any other details as appropriate. If you made a referral, repeat that referral in the letter. If you attempted to refer the client and he or she refused your assistance, renew the offer.

Focus 8: Dual Relationships—Sexual Relationships With Clients

- Do not engage in sexual relationships with current clients. It is also advisable to avoid such relationships with former clients. Know state laws related to this issue.

Self-Awareness as a Key to Avoidance

- Accept the fact that you can become emotionally attracted to a patient, however inappropriate you believe such an attraction to be.
- Do you monitor your feelings toward clients throughout the course of therapy to help you identify inappropriate feelings of attraction toward a patient early on?

Eliminating Confusion About the Therapeutic Relationship

- Even a well-meant word or action can be misinterpreted or can do harm.
- If you use touching consistently and actively in therapy, consider explaining this to the patient and his or her family, if appropriate, before therapy begins.
- Before you touch a patient, consider how that patient will react. Ask yourself:
    1. How well do you know the patient?
    2. Is the patient ready for this kind of contact? (Some clients may never be ready for such contact.)
    3. Could it be misinterpreted by the patient as a sexual overture?
    4. Could it be misinterpreted by the patient's family as a sexual overture?

5. Is touching appropriate in this circumstance?

• Do you think before speaking? Will what you are about to say inappropriately confuse or create apprehension in the client? Ask the same questions that you would ask before touching a patient.

• If a client reacts in a way that alerts you to a potential problem or asks why you behave in a particular way, do you discuss the issue openly and promptly?

Attraction to Clients

• It is the therapist's obligation to maintain a professional relationship with a current client, regardless of the circumstances. It is also advisable to avoid emotional or sexual relationships with former clients.

• If you become emotionally or physically attracted to a client, these feelings will likely interfere with objectivity and therefore may be harmful to the therapeutic process.

• Ask yourself why you are attracted to the client. Are you interpreting your feelings correctly? Is there something about the person that fills a need in yourself?

• Discuss your feelings with an experienced colleague who may be able to help you see your feelings for what they really are or help you recognize when and how your feelings are potentially harmful to both you and the client.

• If your emotions have been influencing the course of therapy in a way that must be changed, you could consider discussing your feelings with the client. However, this should be done only if you can gauge the client's reactions and control your own emotions and reactions in order to avoid an escalation of the situation.

• If you cannot resolve your feelings appropriately, terminate the therapeutic relationship immediately and refer the client to another therapist.

• Seek professional counseling or consultation to help resolve your own emotional feelings about this client.

Attraction to Therapists

• It is not uncommon for clients to develop feelings of attraction toward their therapists.

• It is not the client's responsibility to maintain the professionalism of the relationship.

• Take action, but remember that whatever action you take may have an effect on the client's self-esteem. The success of the client's future treatment may depend on how you handle the situation.

• Do not overreact. Consider the client's actions in relation to the stage of therapy and what those actions may represent. If you decide the client's actions must be confronted directly, develop a plan for dealing with the client's feelings constructively.

• It may be useful to discuss your concerns with an experienced colleague.

• If your patient openly discusses his or her erotic feelings for you or the wish to pursue a sexual relationship, deal with the issue immediately. You might express your recognition of the feelings involved, but at the same time, make it clear that such a relationship would be unethical and potentially harmful to the client. It may be appropriate to discuss transference with the client.

• Support the client in efforts to recognize and deal with his or her feelings, but monitor the situation closely.

• If the client's feelings hinder therapy and progress is not being made, or if those feelings are becoming so extreme as to present a danger to the client's well-being (or your own), it may be necessary to terminate therapy with an appropriate referral.

Considering a Sexual Relationship With a Current or Former Client

• Consider that you may be acting in violation of the ethics of the profession and, in some jurisdictions, of the law.

• Consider whether you should immediately seek treatment for yourself.

• Ask yourself whether you should consider a different profession.

• Remember that you may be sued for sexual misconduct, and be prepared to lose the suit.

If you are in the midst of a therapeutic relationship:

• There is no accepted psychotherapeutic theory or data that supports a sexual relationship, under any circumstances, as being therapeutic. Likewise, none of your respected colleagues will support such therapist–client interactions.

• Ask yourself how your sexual relationship will affect the therapeutic relationship. Can you truthfully say that you will be able to provide quality, objective, healthful care for the client under the circumstances?

• Ask yourself whether you truly are able to conduct yourself in a businesslike manner. (Have you stopped billing the client for services? Are you providing therapy in settings outside the office?)

• Are employees, colleagues, and other clients aware of your sexual relationship? Consider how this knowledge is affecting them. (Such relationships are not likely to remain private for very long.)

• Are you in the sexual relationship out of fear of the repercussions if you terminate it? Or because discontinuation will harm the client emotionally? Or because the client will do physical harm to himself or herself, or even to you? Or because the client will bring an ethics complaint or a malpractice suit against you? Remember that all of these repercussions and others are possible regardless of what you do. Consider discussing the situation with an experienced colleague.

If you consider initiating a relationship with a former client:

• Remember that therapists have been successfully sued for malpractice if such relationships do not work.

• Remember that engaging in a relationship with a former client is illegal in some jurisdictions.

• Consider why the former client underwent therapy and what form of therapy was used. A therapeutic relationship formed during brief therapy aimed at solving a behavioral problem (e.g., a temporary stress reaction) may have less complicated and less enduring effects than, for example, one formed during long-term, intensive therapy, but potential complications must be considered carefully.

- Was therapy terminated by mutual agreement? If you, the client, or both of you felt an attraction before therapy terminated, was therapy ended for an appropriate reason or in order to permit a sexual relationship to develop?
- How long has it been since you treated the client? Is the dependent relationship that existed in therapy no longer present and active? Is there a danger that either of you will fall back into the therapist–client relationship?
- Is it possible that you wish to reestablish the position of power over the client that you held during the therapeutic relationship?
- Is the client still in therapy? How detrimental will the relationship be to his or her progress?
- Does your former client see you as someone other than his or her therapist (or potential therapist)? Are you the kind of person that he or she, if mentally and emotionally healthy, would choose as a partner?
- Will both of you benefit from the relationship? Are your life goals the same?
- It may be helpful to discuss the pending relationship with a colleague prior to initiating it.

In all cases:
- Will there be effects on other family members (e.g., spouses, children)? How will this affect the relationship?

Focus 9: Dual Relationships Other Than Sexual Relationships

- A dual relationship may occur whenever the therapist interacts with the client in more than one capacity, for example, as therapist *and* business partner, guardian, teacher, supervisor, investor, or researcher.
- If a relative, colleague, friend, acquaintance, or other person with whom you have a professional, personal, or social relationship approaches you requesting advice or formal therapy, regardless of the circumstances, such requests may lead to a dual relationship.
- As a professional, other persons' respect for and trust in your knowledge and skill puts you in a position of power over them (even if you are only providing a referral). Choose your actions carefully, remembering that if the action you recommend fails or if you give inappropriate or inadequate advice, harm may be done to others or to yourself.
- It is best to avoid even the appearance of conflict of interest. One's colleagues and others in the community may call your behavior into question.
- Ask yourself what the aim of the relationship would be.
- Have you talked to the other person about the possible repercussions of such a relationship and the dangers of failed expectations and lack of objectivity on both of your parts?
- If appropriate, can you provide a referral to a colleague?
- Do you avoid giving clinical opinions or advice in social settings or casual conversation? Such opinions and advice may be misinterpreted or misused or may even foster ignorance.
- If you find yourself in a dual relationship, do you monitor that relationship closely? Do you evaluate the effectiveness of the therapy in terms of its objectives

and the well-being of both the person undergoing the therapy and yourself as therapist? Attempt to resolve the dual-role nature of the relationship whenever feasible. Terminate the relationship if you see it does not work for either of you.

- Do you avoid the dual-role relationship of providing therapy services to individuals who are or may become your students?
- If you are the only qualified therapist on campus and provide therapy as part of your duties or outside your regular duties, do you refer your own students or close colleagues to another therapist off campus, if one is available?
- If you work in settings where you must provide treatment under circumstances where it may become known that you are treating a specific person—for example, in a rural setting where there are few therapists—do you make a special effort to maintain your client's confidentiality? Should a neighbor question you about your client, do you indicate that his or her well-meaning interest is appreciated but explain the ethics of confidentiality?
- It is never advisable to barter one's services (e.g., provide therapy in return for medical care or real estate advice or professional remodeling). Expectations of both parties in both roles may be difficult to meet or may conflict directly. Also, the laws or standards governing some professions prohibit bartering services under any circumstances.
- Accepting small gifts or tokens of appreciation from a client may be acceptable, but it may also be interpreted as exploitation or undue influence. You should consider the nature of such gifts, the circumstances under which they are given, the client's attitude about what such a gift represents, the frequency with which gifts are given, the clinical implications of the gifts, and so forth.

Interactions With Colleagues

- Do you avoid allowing a personal prejudice to prevent you from providing appropriate support (e.g., a referral, encouragement, consultation) if that colleague has a legitimate need for your assistance?
- Do you avoid forcing your services on a colleague? If he or she needs assistance, particularly when in distress, are you supportive and do you avoid a dual relationship? (See Focus 27.)
- Do you anticipate professional behavior and appropriate service on the part of your colleagues? Do you resolve disputes in a professional manner?
- Do you allow your feelings of friendship or respect for a colleague to overshadow ethical and professional guidelines?

Focus 10: Testing

- Are you familiar with the criteria and guidelines provided in the APA publications, *Standards for Educational and Psychological Testing* (American Educational Research Association, American Psychological Association, and National

Council on Measurement in Education, 1985) and *Guidelines for Computer-Based Tests and Interpretations* (APA Board of Professional Affairs, 1986)?

• Before selecting and using a test, do you consider characteristics of your client that might affect test results, such as age, sex, ethnic and cultural background, and physical impairments (e.g., a hearing impairment might prevent use of an oral test)?

• Assuming that a test is not a measure of language, do you ask whether your client has the language facility necessary to use a written test? Can the client read? Can the client read English? Are there tests available in the client's language?

• Do you know whether the test has been validated with a population that shares the client's characteristics?

• Is there a detailed and accurate manual providing reliability and validity data and explaining how to administer, score, and interpret the results of the test? Do you have a copy?

• To ensure proper use of a test you use repeatedly, is it necessary for you to store unused tests, testing materials, and manuals in a secure place? If so, do you have such a place (e.g., a safe, a locked cabinet) and procedures in place to make sure that security is maintained? Are staff and others who need to be aware of those procedures trained in their use?

• Are you using the most up-to-date, valid, and reliable version of the test? Have you obtained recent information regarding its continued validity and interpretation of results?

• Are you or the person who will administer, score, and interpret the test trained to do so? Is special training required, and if so, how do you obtain that training?

• Even if you are trained to use the test, does its effective use require experience beyond that which you have? If so, consider having the testing done by a more experienced colleague.

• If you are going to use an outside service to score the test, is that service qualified to do so?

Informed Consent and Confidentiality

• Do you explain to your client why you are using the test and how the results will be used? Are you confident that the client has understood your explanation?

• Do you obtain informed consent from the client if you are going to use a colleague or an outside service to provide any portion of the testing service?

• Regardless of the setting, will appropriate steps be taken to maintain the confidentiality of the client's tests?

• If the test is being done at the direction of a third party (e.g., an employer, the court), do you clarify the expectations that that entity has regarding access to and use of test results? Does that party understand your responsibilities regarding the client's confidentiality? Are there any conflicts between the two?

• Does the client understand his or her right to know the results of the test and the right to confidentiality regarding the records of the test in relation to third parties?

Focus 11: Handling Referrals

• Have you developed and do you employ a procedure for receiving and processing referrals? Consider the nature of information to request and the manner in which it should be requested. Do you keep the potential client's sensitivities and vulnerabilities in mind?

• Are you specific about information you will provide over the telephone prior to meeting a client? This might include office hours, fees and payment plans (including acceptance of insurance), and similar factual information.

• If your staff receives referrals for you, have you trained your staff in handling referrals and in maintaining client privacy and confidentiality?

• If the individual who refers a client to you is a mental health, medical health, or other professional, do you seek the client's consent to consult with the referral source? If possible, do you consult with the referral source regarding why the referral was made prior to seeing the client? It might also be useful to review the client's file.

• If the client does not consent, do you document the fact in the record?

First Client Contact

• Do you always note the name, address, and telephone numbers of the potential client and the source of the referral?

• Do you identify the reason the client is seeking therapy?

• When you set up an initial appointment, do you explain that the session will be devoted to your gaining an understanding of the problem(s) and to discussing what might be involved in the therapeutic contract, if you use such devices?

• Do you make detailed notes regarding this initial contact and any follow-up consultation you have with the referring professional?

If a colleague or another professional contacts you first:

• Obtain basically the same information that you do when the client initiates contact.

Providing a Referral

• If the individual is not a client and you do not intend to treat him or her as a client, solicit no more information than necessary to provide an appropriate referral.

• If you are going to speak to the professional to whom you are referring a client, obtain the client's consent.

• If you are requesting special services for a client from a colleague, provide the colleague with only the necessary information to support the goals of the referral.

• If you are terminating therapy with a client and he or she is continuing in therapy with another therapist, review the client's file. Identify and summarize information that should be shared with the new therapist, or select pertinent documents that would be appropriate to provide to the new therapist. Before providing information or conferring with the new therapist, obtain the client's permission.

- Record pertinent information relating to the referral in the client's file, including the nature of information provided to colleagues, the results of the referral, and so forth.

Focus 12: Undue Influence

- It is possible for you to unintentionally influence a client in an inappropriate way. Be alert to your influence over your clients.
- Observe clients' responses to you closely.
- Consider the degree to which transference has occurred.
- Ask the following questions:
  1. How compliant is the client to suggestions that I make?
  2. Does he or she insist that I provide rules and specific instructions beyond what may be necessary to support successful therapy?
- Do not impose your beliefs on clients who may not believe as you do, or consciously attempt to alter a client's beliefs simply because you do not agree with a particular life-style.
- In marital, couples, and family therapy, fully inform clients and, if appropriate, family members and significant others of the potential risks (and benefits) to existing relationships.
- When treating children, are you sensitive to the potential reactions of parents or guardians to changes that may occur in the client's relationship with them? Do you have a session with the child and his or her parents or guardian before therapy begins to explain what may happen as therapy progresses?
- Do you avoid even the appearance of conflict of interest (personal involvement, socializing, accepting gifts, etc.)? You should not permit clients to make bequests to you.
- Are you alert to undue influence by others (e.g., coercion by the family to make the client participate in therapy)?

Inappropriate Influence

- *By you.* Do you take steps to assist the client in gaining independence? Do you discuss indications of dependency with the client and include overcoming it as a therapy goal? If the problem persists and inhibits therapy, do you consider referring the client to an appropriate colleague?
- *By others.* Consider the impact of the influence. Does it inhibit the client's progress? Is he or she aware of it? Is it an appropriate topic for discussion with the client or with the person or persons influencing the client? Would a joint session be helpful or damaging?
- Do you document your observations and efforts in the client's file?

Focus 13: Danger and the Duty To Warn or Protect

- You should educate yourself regarding the standards of practice and laws and regulations concerning danger and your duty to warn or protect family members, friends, legal authorities, and pertinent others (a) if you believe that a client may pose a threat to himself or herself or to any other person or (b) if you have specific knowledge of a criminal act planned by a client.
- Potential dangers to the client include not only physical harm to himself or herself (e.g., self-mutilation, suicide) and others but also self-negligence (e.g., failing to eat, danger of alcohol narcosis).
- Learn the conditions associated with suicidal tendencies and violence against others and learn to recognize the warning signs and symptoms of violent acts by a client with those conditions.
- Do you maintain careful documentation of a client's threats against oneself and others and of the steps you take to intervene? Are you alert for patterns of behavior indicating a potential for violence as well as for overt and realizable threats?
- Consider the following when evaluating potential dangerousness:
    1. Does the client have a history of impulsiveness, verbal or physical violence toward himself or herself or others, buying or using weapons, substance abuse, volatile temper?
    2. Does the client have a history of affective illness (e.g., depression, psychosis)?
    3. Does the client believe that he or she has a reason to seek revenge or to do harm to another?
    4. Are there aspects of the client's life situation—active drug use, perceived reason to attack another (e.g., jealousy of a partner, anger at another person), recent divorce, and so forth—that could contribute to the client acting out against others or himself or herself?
    5. Is the client taking one or more medications that could interact in a negative way or have side effects that could create or aggravate existing upset?
    6. Is the threat real or being made for effect or to avoid some other consequence (e.g., arrest or imprisonment, loss of a spouse)?
    7. Does the client have the means to carry out the threat?
    8. Does the client have access to the threatened person or place?
- Consider questioning others, with your client's permission, who may have knowledge of the client's actions and intentions. If the client refuses to provide a release, consider the risks (e.g., loss of the client's trust) and benefits (e.g., protection of the client) of violating the client's right to confidentiality. It is always wise to review state and federal laws and regulations regarding release or solicitation of information without consent.
- Do you work with the client to help him or her overcome the impulse to act out violently? Do you help the person to express feelings of anger and upset openly, to identify the source of upset, and to attempt to resolve it without violence?
- Even if the client professes to have set aside his or her intentions to do harm, are you alert for signs that the client has not done so?

- Do you consult with an experienced colleague if you are uncertain as to the seriousness of a client's threat of suicide, assault on another person, commission of a crime, kidnapping, or similar endangerment to another person?
- Request the aid of a physician should it appear necessary to provide medication to the client.
- Consider whether it is necessary to remove the client from a potentially harmful environment to a place of safety (e.g., a shelter).
- Consider whether it is necessary to institutionalize the client (see Focus 14). Consider the following in making such a decision:
  1. Has the client failed to respond to hospitalization in the past?
  2. Does the client need close monitoring or other treatments offered in a hospital, and is it likely that hospitalization will be effective on this occasion?
  3. Could it worsen the client's condition?
  4. Are there no other effective less intrusive options?

Protecting Others and Yourself

- If you believe that the client is serious about the intention to commit suicide or to do other harm to himself or herself or to others and believe that he or she has the means to do so, alert the client's guardian or the appropriate authorities, or both. Consider whether it is appropriate to inform concerned relatives or friends in light of laws and ethical principles related to the client's confidentiality rights.
- If the health or life of another person is threatened by your client and you believe that the client has both the will and the means to act on that threat, contact that person or the appropriate authorities, or both.
- Protect yourself. Your position and skills may not be sufficient to protect you if a client threatens you. Do not assume that you can talk him or her out of it or that you can protect yourself. Stay alert and take measures to protect yourself, in as well as out of your office, if you believe it to be necessary.

Focus 14: Commitment

- Know the laws and regulations in your state that are pertinent to voluntary and involuntary commitment.
- If a client's condition begins to deteriorate, consider consulting with appropriate colleagues, if necessary, in a timely fashion.
- Consider whether there is a possible physical cause for the client's condition. Could the behavior be drug-induced? Could there be an organic cause? Have a medical examination conducted if appropriate.
- If the behavior is drug-induced, how long will the effects last? Is temporary hospitalization an option for that period? If so, under what conditions? How closely should the client be monitored? What should be done after the initial period of detoxification or withdrawal? Would continued commitment be appropriate?

- Consider what your goals are in recommending commitment. Is the client dangerous to himself or herself or others? Has the client threatened or attempted suicide? Is the client in an environment that fails to protect him or her from harm or that causes harm? Is the client unable to care for himself or herself? Is the client in need of care but unable to request treatment of the kind provided in a mental health facility or outpatient setting? (Not all jurisdictions allow commitment because of inability to care for oneself or because treatment is needed but the client cannot request it.)

- Consider alternatives to commitment carefully before choosing commitment as the only option. Would the client improve under a different treatment program or treatment modality? Would referral to another therapist for evaluation or treatment be advisable?

- Has the client been hospitalized previously? Was hospitalization effective or not?

- How will commitment (or even the discussion of commitment) affect the client's attitude toward you as a therapist and toward therapy in general? If the client's progress is likely to be inhibited, is it likely that the negative effect can be overcome in time? If not, is the client's condition such that, regardless of the circumstances, there is no choice but to commit?

- Would the hospitalization be voluntary? Is the client capable of, competent to, and willing to admit himself or herself? What are the laws governing release under such circumstances and how important are they in terms of the client's condition? (Can the client terminate self-commitment at any time, regardless of the circumstances of his or her condition?)

- If hospitalization is involuntary, what procedural steps must be followed under the laws in your state?

- If you are considering requesting that the court authorize a client's involuntary commitment, consider what you will do should the request for commitment be denied and you strongly believe that commitment is necessary to prevent harm to the client or others. Is it possible to appeal the decision? What happens if the appeal is denied? What steps are you required to take—both legally and ethically regardless of the ethic of confidentiality—to warn potential victims of possible danger or to alert police authorities?

- Be sure that you can demonstrate the need for commitment under legal and therapeutic criteria.

Preparing for Commitment

- How is hospitalization likely to affect the client initially? Will it induce further withdrawal, increase violence, or in other ways aggravate the client's condition and behavior? What information does the staff of the facility need to have to be prepared for this?

- Consider how much you should explain to the client. How much is the client able to understand? Is he or she competent to understand the personal, family, and legal ramifications of commitment?

- Before proceeding with commitment, consider how to prepare the family or significant others involved for what will occur during and after the process of commitment. How will you explain what the client's likely initial reaction will be, how he or she is likely to behave once committed, and so forth?
- Is there a choice about which facility the client will enter? If so, which facility is the most appropriate for your client? If there are several options, how involved should the client or the client's family or guardian be in selecting the appropriate facility? What are the criteria that should be applied in that selection?

Focus 15: Care of Institutionalized Clients

- The services that a psychologist is allowed to provide in institutionalized settings may be limited by law, regulation, or specific privileges granted to the psychologist by a hospital. Be sure that you understand such restrictions, and any special requirements of an institution, before providing treatment in an institutional setting.
- Institutionalized clients have rights, even though laws and regulations governing institutionalization may restrict those rights to some degree.
- Many states have enacted a bill of rights for recipients of mental health services. Be sure you are familiar with such statutes.
- Clients who are institutionalized are particularly vulnerable because of their lack of physical freedom and the severity of their condition, and in some instances because of possible exposure to physical and emotional harm from inadequately trained or supervised staff or residents within an institution. Be alert and take steps to protect your client if necessary.
- Institutionalization does not imply helplessness. Work to dispel such beliefs in yourself and your client. Your client should be allowed to function as normally as possible—to have an opportunity to work and be paid for work, to make decisions independently, to participate in decisions regarding his or her treatment, and to engage actively in living. The more actively involved the client is, the more likely it is that he or she will adjust more effectively and quickly when he or she reenters the community.
- Be sensitive to your own attitudes and feelings toward institutionalized care and its effects on clients, and work to overcome inappropriate resistance or guilt about the limitations institutionalization places on clients.
- If a client has voluntarily admitted himself or herself, he or she may have the right to leave the institution at any time within specified time periods. Do you understand the legal and regulatory strictures governing voluntary institutionalization?
- Involuntary commitment may be requested by family members or guardians; however, it must be ordered by the court. Laws governing commitment by the court or by others may differ significantly. Involuntary commitment is a legal decision, not a psychological or medical decision.
- Do you inform yourself about the specific nature of an institutionalized client's commitment and the required period of confinement as well as the terms of release?

- Do you obtain advice as needed from experienced colleagues, supervisors, legal counsel, and others?
- Have you considered the importance of families in the treatment of institutionalized clients? In some instances, a client's progress may be influenced greatly, for good or ill, by the active participation of families or relatives in group or individual therapy. Also, the client's treatment can be enhanced by their active support of therapy.
- Have you considered the effects on families of their relatives' confinement and, especially, on those whose relatives have a chronic mental illness? Within the limitations set by state law regarding confidentiality, do you keep family members informed about the progress of their relatives? If necessary, do you provide them with referrals for therapy, or, if it does not represent a conflict of interest, do you provide them with therapy yourself?
- When an institutionalized client reenters the community, the understanding, stability, and mental well-being of his or her family will be critical in the client's continued improvement. Do you take steps to educate the family and to prepare them for supporting the client?

Institutionalized Clients' Rights

- Institutionalized clients are entitled to receive protection of their civil rights, such as the rights to marry, vote, and so forth. The degree of freedom allowed in the exercise of those rights may be limited by law or by the client's condition. The client or his or her guardian should be clearly informed of the client's rights and of possible restrictions of those rights. Institutionalization is not synonymous with incompetency.
- The institutionalized client is entitled to receive prompt, appropriate care, including evaluation before medications are given.
- The institutionalized client is entitled to treatment planned and provided by qualified staff, including periodic review and evaluation, as well as to treatment aimed at returning the client to the community as soon as possible, if possible.
- The institutionalized client is entitled to privacy, including physical privacy within the limits available (e.g., clients treated in wards should have access to private storage of personal belongings) and secure storage of their records.
- The institutionalized client is entitled to have visitors and to communicate with family and others outside the institution. The facility should provide access to telephones, if they are appropriate considering the client's condition, and should permit the exchange of letters. If you have reason to believe that a client is a danger to others, it may be necessary to screen outgoing mail.

Medication

- Medication can be prescribed and administered only under the supervision of a physician and only by licensed personnel. If you believe that a client requires medication, consult with a physician and other colleagues as appropriate, but examine alternatives to medication before requesting it for a client.

• If the client refuses a particular form of treatment (e.g., medication, individual therapy), consider how to discuss his or her reasons for refusal and explain the value or necessity of the treatment in improving the client's condition. If alternative treatments are available, discuss their risks and benefits, but only provide alternative treatment if you believe that it will benefit the client.

• Should the client continue to refuse needed treatment, consider whether it is necessary *and* legal to impose the treatment on the client and, if so, how the client would respond under such circumstances.

• If the client's acceptance of treatment would be increased if he or she were treated by another therapist, consider how you will discuss this with the client and how you will transfer the client to the care of another qualified therapist.

Issues Surrounding Discharge

• If a client wishes, against your advice, to leave the hospital and can legally do so, consider whether to arrange for involuntary commitment (with permission of a guardian or by court order). Carefully document the competency evaluation of the client, the reasons that institutionalization should continue, the reasons that alternative treatments would not be effective, and the expected results of continued institutionalized care. Make sure you are familiar with your state law on the criteria and procedures for involuntary commitment.

• Are you familiar with community resources that will be available to the client after he or she is discharged and the support that will be available from the client's family and friends?

• As a client improves, begin to plan for his or her discharge. Prior to discharge, develop a mutual agreement regarding termination of care and appropriate plans for follow-up that may be needed.

• Do you take particular care in evaluating the appropriateness of discharge of clients who presented a danger to themselves or others prior to or during institutionalization? Consider the laws and regulations governing release and the alternatives for necessary continued care and support available to the client in the community. Keep in mind your obligation to protect others and the community.

Focus 16: Physical Assault and Emotional and Physical Abuse

• Regardless of the laws governing such situations, it is your ethical obligation to protect, if possible, individuals who are or who may be victims of physical, emotional, and psychological abuse.

• If a client—even one with extreme paranoia or a history of fabricating stories—indicates that he or she has been assaulted by a family member, another mental health professional, another person in a mental institution, or any other person, do not dismiss such claims (or believe them) based on assumptions about the client's condition.

• Ask yourself whether your subjective and emotional responses to situations of abuse or your beliefs regarding who commits abuse and the reasons that they commit abuse blind you to indicators that abuse has occurred or to indicators about who committed the abuse. At the same time, do not be blind to the possibility that abuse may not have occurred.

- Are you familiar with the signs and symptoms of possible abuse and the effects of abuse even if you do not wish to undertake treatment of abuse victims?
- Do you know the laws that govern the reporting of the suspected abuse of children, spouses, the mentally disabled, and the elderly? Do you know and understand the legal and ethical limits covering confidentiality, privilege, and liability in situations where abuse may be present?
- If appropriate, consider questioning the client directly to obtain information.
- If appropriate, consider discussing your concerns with a parent or guardian or with another individual with knowledge of the client's living circumstances, but *be cautious.* You may believe that you know who victimized the client, but it is sometimes difficult to determine who is the abuser.
- If in doubt, consider obtaining an independent evaluation by a qualified colleague.
- If you report an incident of possible abuse, do you follow up the report to see what action was taken? If you are not satisfied with that action, should you consider taking further steps within the ethics and laws governing your actions?
- Do you treat victims of abuse if you do not have appropriate expertise? Consider referring the client to an experienced colleague.
- If you do not have suitable training but choose to treat the individual, consider doing so under the supervision of an experienced colleague. It is advisable to obtain the client's informed consent to undertake treatment under such circumstances.
- Do you carefully document the results of your evaluation of possible abuse and the actions that you take as a result of it? Such a record could include information on what led you to suspect abuse and why you did or *did not* act upon those suspicions. Note the response and action taken by authorities and others if you reported the abuse.

Focus 17: Providing Pro Bono and Volunteer Services

- Regardless of whether you receive payment or have a formalized relationship with an organization, the psychological services you provide will be judged both according to the accepted ethics and practice guidelines governing the profession and under the laws governing practice.
- In general, the practice guidelines that apply to treatment of your regular clients are equally applicable to pro bono or volunteer services.
- Organizations to which you provide volunteer services as a psychologist should comply with the ethics, guidelines, and laws governing psychological practice.
- If you provide pro bono services to clients, maintain complete and accurate records of the number of sessions you have provided and of all other relevant client information, as you would for any client.

- The amount of time spent in volunteer services should be considered in light of caseload and other obligations and of how your clients may be affected. Consider whether you are able to make the appropriate investment of time and quality of services that the organization has requested.
- Avoid offering volunteer services if your sole purpose is self-aggrandizement (i.e., ego fulfillment, self-advertisement).
- Consider whether you are qualified to provide requested services. If necessary, consult an experienced colleague for advice or tutelage, or refer the organization to a qualified colleague who is willing to volunteer.
- If you are providing pro bono services to a court or other institution that has highly specialized requirements, become familiar with both the general requirements and the specific procedures that must be followed.

Focus 18: Running a Professional Office

- You are ethically responsible and may be held legally responsible for the actions others take on your behalf. Carefully choose all employees, including those who provide support services such as accounting, answering services, and bill collection; those with whom you consult or from whom you obtain evaluations and other psychology-related services (e.g., testing); and others upon whom your professionalism and the client's well-being may depend.
- Have you obtained appropriate advice regarding professional business practices such as accounting and billing, tax records and preparation, contracts, file maintenance, and so forth?
- Do you know what the business licensing and reporting requirements are in your community and state? There may also be requirements that govern how you set up your office (e.g., you may be required to have a separate door through which clients may enter without going through a residence). Have you obtained required licenses and renewals?
- If your office is in your home, consider whether to have a separate phone line for business calls. Inform family members of how calls on that line (or calls received on family phones) should be handled in your absence.
- If you are using an answering service, select carefully and provide them with specific instructions regarding client calls and procedures for emergencies. Be sure to alert the service when you will be absent or unavailable. Be alert to complaints clients may make regarding how their calls are handled.
- If you use a telephone answering machine, it is advisable to have one that provides for playback of messages when you call in. You should check your machine frequently for messages from clients.
- Your office practices and environment should reflect your professionalism. Expect employees to behave as professionals. Conduct your business in a businesslike manner, maintaining appropriate records and following appropriate practices for billing and other activities. Furnish your office comfortably and attractively, but remember that it is not a home.
- If you provide services in an unusual setting or under unusual circumstances (e.g., in a jail, group therapy in your living room), make sure that your clients

understand that the setting is incidental to your role as a professional. Clearly establish the ground rules so that a professional relationship is maintained.

• If you are confused, do not know how to handle a particular situation, or doubt your ability to do so, discuss the problem with a colleague with more experience or specific expertise in the area in question. Contact local, state, and national professional groups for information and guidance. If necessary, seek professional advice (from a lawyer, consultant, or personal therapist, as appropriate). Remember: However puzzling, unusual, or embarrassing a situation may be in your experience, it is highly unlikely that it is universally unique.

Managing a Staff

• The well-being of clients and the effectiveness with which you practice depends, in part, upon the attitude and abilities of your staff.

• Do you know the employment regulations that are pertinent where you practice? Do you comply with those regulations, particularly in regard to payment of unemployment compensation; required benefits such as insurance; all matters related to taxes; and so forth?

• Have you obtained supervisory training for yourself if you have limited or no experience in supervising employees? Supervising staff is different than supervising students and conducting therapy.

• Do you select staff carefully? Do you seek past employment records prior to hiring new staff? You can be held accountable for the actions of your staff. If you have failed to do a proper employment evaluation of a staff person who subsequently harms one of your patients, you may be held liable.

• Do you train staff carefully? Do you place particular emphasis on maintaining client confidentiality and on what to say and not to say to clients under normal and emergency circumstances?

• Do you document procedures? Are all staff members trained in both everyday and emergency procedures? Do they have access to the written procedures as needed? If you are operating without a staff, it is particularly useful to note how you handle procedures.

• Do you observe and evaluate staff performance? You should note the following:

1. How do they deal with clients?
2. How do they interact with organizations and individuals who are referral sources for your practice?
3. Do they behave professionally at all times?
4. Do they handle records appropriately?
5. Do they prepare billing records accurately and promptly?

• It is useful to set up written criteria for performance (e.g., job descriptions) to which staff can refer when they are being trained and as they work. It may be appropriate to prepare written evaluations.

• If an employee is not behaving appropriately or performing adequately, do you provide prompt feedback? Remember that the well-being of clients and your own practice are at stake. Do you terminate employees promptly if they are unable or unwilling to provide the service required?

Fees, Billing, and Bill Collection

• For your client's well-being and your own, consider establishing the client's ability to pay for services before services begin.

• Do you know and follow laws governing billing and bill collection in your state and locality?

• If you are considering receiving or paying referral fees, are you familiar with state and federal laws regarding such fees? Also, there may be Federal Trade Commission regulations that are pertinent to your practice. Do you know them?

• Do you have specific policies for charging and collecting fees? Do you inform clients fully about these policies? Are you meticulous in their implementation? It may be useful to remind clients of the policies periodically. It may also be useful to provide a written copy of the policies when you begin therapy.

• Do you request prompt payment? Do you avoid allowing a client's bills to accumulate? Do you make special payment arrangements if necessary?

• If you have established a scale of fees, do you have criteria for applying the scale? Are you thoughtful in how you implement those criteria? Can you justify why you charge or do not charge a client a specific fee?

• When you refer a client for evaluation or other services as part of your services, do you make sure that he or she is aware of separate charges that will be made for those services before they are provided?

• Do you obtain and retain appropriate information regarding each client's insurance?

• Do you train employees thoroughly in how to receive and record payments in the form of checks and cash? You and your employees should handle payments consistently at all times.

• Do you periodically review billing and collection procedures and determine the accuracy with which they are followed? Do you make adjustments as necessary?

• Consider carefully how you use collection agencies. Do you use such agencies only when necessary? Do you select agencies with great care? Do you provide no more information than necessary (e.g., amount owed) to protect the client's right to privacy? Do you alert the client before turning over the account for collection? Using collection agencies or attempting to collect an outstanding balance due can result in malpractice litigation against you, especially if the client failed to pay for services that he or she felt were unsatisfactory, unhelpful, or incompetent.

• Do you avoid using confidential information you have obtained about a client during therapy or in your position as a professional in an attempt to collect payment? Do you refrain from threatening a client with the possible release of confidential information in order to collect fees?

• Are you cautious if you are considering terminating a client because he or she has not paid a bill? Do you try to negotiate a payment plan or discuss alternative rates?

- If the client must be terminated, do you refer the client for any needed services?
- Unpaid accounts should not be treated as pro bono work. They are bad debts. If you *choose* to treat a client at no charge, before treatment begins or at any time thereafter during treatment, then that would be pro bono work.

Focus 19: Record Keeping

- Your records should include both accurate client records and thorough, accurate business records.
- Records can both protect you or be used against you in malpractice litigation. Not keeping records does not provide a defense. In fact, such a practice may be considered a breach of practice guidelines. In hospital practice it is often said, "If it isn't written down, it didn't happen."
- Never falsify records.
- Never withhold records that must be provided to others under the law.
- Do you maintain control over all records, especially those of clients? Do you keep records in a secure place? If you have a staff, have you established thorough guidelines on secure and ethical record handling and record keeping?

Client Files

- Regarding ownership, in most settings, psychologists own their own files. In others (e.g., institutions), the files may legally belong to an employer. Do you know the law or rulings related to ownership? Do you know the law related to clients' rights to the information in their files?
- Do you understand the value and purpose of record keeping in the management of a case or in reporting on its management?
  1. Records provide a foundation for the proper diagnosis and treatment as well as for the future care of a client.
  2. Records can assist in preparing you for testimony in cases where expert testimony is needed.
  3. Records can provide factual information on a case requiring evidence of meeting the standards of care.
- Do you maintain a separate file on each client?
- Are you clear in your own mind about why you are making a note? Are you detailing the progress of the case (e.g., your plan for treatment, mileposts in treatment, goals) or observations and interpretations of what is transpiring?
- Do you clearly identify what is fact (e.g., test data, specific observations of behavior), what is interpretation or theory (e.g., implications of test data, implications of behavior), and what is hearsay from others?
- Do you identify in the file the origin of interpretive information that you did not originate that may be pertinent to treatment (e.g., a teacher commented on a child's behavior, a nurse made an observation about an institutionalized client's behavior pattern)?

- Are you sensitive to the implications of what you record? Ask yourself whether what you are considering recording and the way in which you are considering entering the information is pertinent and helpful to treatment and whether it is potentially embarrassing or harmful to the client. Remember that the client or a third party at some time may obtain legal access to the file.
- Include the following basic information, as appropriate:
  1. name
  2. address
  3. home and office telephone numbers
  4. telephone number of someone to contact should an emergency incapacitate the client
  5. date of first contact with the client and nature of contact (e.g., phone call)
  6. if the client was referred, name of referral source and reason for referral
  7. demographic data (age, sex, ethnic group if pertinent)
  8. family data (marital status, children, other information if pertinent)
  9. special information such as recent immigrant status, impairment of sight or hearing, and other physical or special difficulties that might pose a barrier to treatment or cause the client stress
  10. observations about the individual's language facility if relevant (e.g., the client does not speak English, cannot read)
  11. details regarding mental health insurance
  12. medical history (pertinent illnesses and treatment)
  13. history of substance use, including use of prescription medications (with dosages), current medications taken, use of over-the-counter drugs, patterns of abuse, and history of treatment received
  14. use of alcohol and nature of use; patterns of abuse and history of treatment received
  15. name of the client's personal physician, if known
- Ongoing record keeping should include, as appropriate:
  1. dates of all meetings with the client
  2. billing and payment history
  3. documents such as contracts and consent forms
  4. names of individuals with whom you formally consult about the client, including reasons for consultation and dates
  5. test materials and scoring data
  6. record of all contacts (oral and written) between you and the client and between you and others regarding the client
- In recording treatments, do you note the alternatives you considered; risks and benefits of treatments considered; why a specific treatment was chosen; treatment goals and anticipated outcomes; techniques used; and what you told or did not tell the client about that treatment and why you may have withheld information, if you did?
- Are you methodical and consistent in keeping case files? Do you set a time each day (e.g., at the end of the day or in the 15 minutes between sessions) to annotate records of sessions with clients? Delay can create confusion and introduce error.

- Have you a set time to review files periodically to allow yourself to add subsequent information and obtain a broader (or more specific) picture of patterns of behavior and treatment?
- When contact with a client or others about the client is by phone, do you record the details of that contact (date, time, reason for contact, who initiated call, notations on what transpired)?
- Do you record even apparently casual contact with the client (e.g, chance meeting on the street) noting date, time, nature of contact, and what transpired? Even casual contacts can become important at a later date.
- Should you keep two sets of case notes? Know the local and state laws and consumer laws regarding record keeping and access to records. Separating the formal record (which theoretically includes objective information about a case) from your personal file (which theoretically includes subjective information) may protect your privilege as a professional or the client's right to confidentiality under certain circumstances. However, consider both the law and the needs of the client. Formal files are typically subject to subpoena; a psychologist's personal notes may not be.

Record Retention

- Laws governing record retention may vary from place to place as well as in relation to the type of record. Do you know the laws governing client file retention (likely to be governed by state law, although federal regulations may be in place in some settings) and business record retention (possibly governed by federal and state law)?
- *Client files*. It is recommended (in *Specialty Guidelines for the Delivery of Services*) that you (a) retain full records (including records of court-related actions and transactions with insurance companies) for 3 years after termination and full records or summaries of records for an additional 12 years after that and (b) that you do not destroy records any sooner than 15 years after you last see the client. Some psychologists recommend that you retain full records perpetually.
- *Business records*. In most instances, retain business records according to guidelines provided by the federal government (i.e., Internal Revenue Service), unless state law requires a longer period of retention.

Focus 20: Providing Information to the Client and to Third Parties

- The client has the right to information in his or her file. In some circumstances (e.g., institutional settings), the records may not be your property. Be alert to changes in laws governing the access of clients and others to client records.
- If a client is not competent, he or she may be unable to provide legal consent. However, the client may have the legal right to be informed about and consent to the release of information within the limits of his or her understanding.

Client Consent To Release Information

- Whenever possible, do you obtain the client's written consent to release information from his or her records, even when that information is provided to the client? Do you make sure that the client understands the implications of releasing the information?
- If oral consent is acceptable in an emergency, do you still document the details of such consent carefully?
- If information is provided without consent (e.g., in emergencies, under subpoena), do you take steps to ameliorate potential harm to the client, and, if appropriate, do you discuss related issues with the client to help overcome any loss of trust in you by the client?
- Before providing information under court order or legal requirement (subpoena), do you consider carefully whether it violates the client's right to confidentiality and how it will affect the client? Do you seek legal advice regarding actions you might take if you feel it necessary to withhold information? Do you always seek the client's permission before releasing any information?
- Do you avoid discussing the client's treatment with a client's family member, friend, or even the client's guardian without the client's knowledge, even when that individual participates in therapy with the client?
- Do you provide only required information about a client to consultants or those providing services, and only with the express permission of the client?
- Do you avoid discussing identifiable and specific information about a client in casual conversation, even with another psychologist?
- Do you avoid publishing, in oral or written form, specific and identifiable information about a client? If a case is unique, even if it appears to be sufficiently disguised, it may be advisable to discuss using it with the client and to obtain the client's consent to use the information.
- Do you know the circumstances under which oral statements made by you or the client in the presence of a third party (e.g., a nurse) may void the legal protection of the client's confidentiality? Pay particular attention to laws and rulings related to this.
- Do you know the laws related to confidentiality in group therapy? If a client is considering participating in group therapy, do you warn the client when information shared in group therapy is not protected by law?

Requests for Information

- When a client or third party requests information, do you:
  1. ask for and discuss the reason for the request?
  2. consider the extent of information required?
  3. consider how to organize and convey the information?
  4. provide only the minimum factual data required?
  5. communicate in writing rather than by phone, or confirm in writing as soon as possible information provided in emergencies by phone?

6. review with the client the details of a third-party request and your response, and obtain consent to release the information?

- Before providing information requested by the client or a third party, consider whether there is good reason to withhold the information (e.g., to protect the client or comply with the law). If so, explain this to the client if appropriate. Clients will rarely be denied access to the information contained in their records.

- If a colleague requests information about a client, evaluate the reasons for the request. If there is an emergency or the client is unable to provide the information or consent, provide information if and only if such release is permitted by law and if withholding it will endanger the client.

Providing Accurate Information

- Do not falsify information at the request of a client, regardless of the circumstances surrounding the request. Discuss with the client the issues and implications of such a request, including its legality.

- Do not falsify information you provide to a client at his or her request. If there is potential harm to the client, explain this to the client. If it is possible to summarize the information in a way that will not confuse or harm the client, do so. It is sometimes useful to sit down with the client to review the file, being sure to explain the nature of the contents and the method of taking notes.

- Do not release information provided to you by another source; if appropriate, refer the request to the party providing the information.

- Never alter or destroy permanent records in order to withhold information.

- If it is necessary to clarify a point in a record, the correction should be noted as such and kept in chronological order. Do not erase, write over, white out, or otherwise alter earlier entries.

Release Forms

- The following issues could be included in a release form:
    1. name of party requesting information
    2. date of release
    3. purpose of request
    4. information to be released
    5. how information will be used
    6. date at which the release is no longer valid
    7. statement that the client may revoke the release at any time
    8. the client's signature acknowledging the request and the proposed use of the information
    9. statement that consent covers only information provided in response to the specific request (i.e., for one-time use only).

Focus 21: Filing Insurance Reimbursement Requests

- The professional relationship exists between the therapist and the client, not the therapist and the insurance company. The client should be responsible to the therapist for payment of services and the insurance company responsible to the client for reimbursement of costs.

- Are you familiar with special laws and regulations in your state related to (a) who may legally receive reimbursement under health insurance policies and (b) the nature of services that can be provided in special settings such as health maintenance organizations or private practitioner organizations?

- Do you maintain the client's confidentiality and right to informed consent at all times when dealing with insurance companies or others who have oversight over the client's insurance coverage? If it is necessary to contact a third party (whether that party is the company, an employer, or an insurance policyholder), do you obtain the client's written consent before contacting that third party?

- Do not falsify claims filed with insurance companies. Falsification of information may lead to criminal prosecution or to a civil suit.

- Are you familiar with the requirements of the client's insurance company for information regarding treatment (and its relation to the ethics of confidentiality and privilege)? If you have questions, do you clarify them before filing a claim?

- Obtain from the client (or from the insurance company's literature or representative) and record for future reference the following information about the client's insurance:

    1. name and address of the employer (if the insurance is employer-provided)
    2. name and address of the insurance company
    3. policyholder's name and address and relationship to the client
    4. group or individual policy and identification numbers
    5. date of the insurance contract
    6. appropriate address to send the claim
    7. typical period between filing and payment
    8. nature of coverage
    9. type of policy (e.g., family, individual)
    10. limitations of coverage (e.g., what conditions are not covered)
    11. service settings covered
    12. services covered (in addition to mental health)
    13. percentage of cost covered
    14. maximum amount paid per session and in total and for what period overall
    15. the amount of the deductible and whether it has been met
    16. whether the company will pay you directly
    17. whether the company accepts (or requires) the use of numerical codes for diagnoses or treatments and the source of those codes

- Will another company or the client be providing copayments? Do laws or regulations limit copayments? What are the issues regarding collecting or forgoing such payments?

- Do you verify the client's coverage, if necessary, by calling the insurance company or (if possible without violating confidentiality) the client's employer or the policyholder?
- Do you use the insurance company's own claim form (preferable because a company may require special information not required by other companies) or a standard form approved by the state insurance commission?
- Do you maintain a record of all insurance claims information along with other information on the client's case? Do you retain copies of all claims filed and carefully record payments received in the client's records?
- It is good business practice to review files periodically to identify claims that are inappropriately delayed and to inquire about their status.

Denied Claims

- Claims are often denied because:
    1. information is missing (e.g., policy number, signature, code numbers)
    2. services or conditions are not covered
    3. premiums are not paid
    4. the policy is invalid in the state in which services are provided
    5. the claim was not filed within the time limit allowed.
- If it is not provided, do you request detailed information about why the claim was denied?
- Do you refile claims with the additional information, assuming that providing that information does not violate standards of confidentiality?
- If the information requested would violate the client's confidentiality, do you inform the company of this circumstance, perhaps providing alternative information that might meet the company's needs? If the claim is still denied, it may be necessary to file a complaint with the state insurance commission, providing details about the claim and any special circumstances.
- If you know that the client is legally entitled to receive payment under the policy and the company continues to deny the claim, do you write the company setting out the laws that make the claim legitimate, reiterating the eligibility of the claim, and requesting payment? If the company continues to deny legitimate payment, the client may file a complaint with the state insurance commission, providing details regarding the claim and the attempts made to recover payment.

Focus 22: Marketing Your Services

- Are you familiar with the guidelines relevant to advertising that are provided by boards and committees of the American Psychological Association (e.g., *Marketing Psychological Services: A Practitioner's Guide*; APA Board of Professional Affairs, 1986) and with state law and Federal Trade Commission regulations?
- Consult with an experienced colleague or relevant organization if you have questions about the ethics of a specific advertising approach.

- Do you ensure that all advertising is based on information that is valid and accurate? Do you advertise only the credentials that you have, the services that you do offer, and fee schedules that are accurate? Do you make sure that advertisements do not mislead or deceive potential clients?
- Do you use language that potential clients can understand?
- It is ethical to use media advertising (newspapers, magazines, radio, television).
- Psychologists serving organizations, corporations, and businesses may have more latitude in the approaches they use in advertising, but they should take special care to be accurate in advertising their competence in brochures and other materials.

Focus 23: The Psychologist as an Employee and Special Settings

Portions of this checklist were adapted from "Guidelines for Conditions of Employment of Psychologists" (APA Committee on Academic Freedom and Conditions of Employment, 1987).

- As an employee, you must be licensed as required by law and must have the appropriate training to provide the services for which you are hired.
- Are you sensitive to the employment practices of a potential employer? Employers should hire only qualified professionals and support staff, should adhere to equal opportunity employment practices, and should follow appropriate recruitment procedures for full-time, part-time, temporary, and nonstandard positions. Conditions of employment should be truthfully and fully explained by the employer.
- Are you truthful regarding the nature of your credentials and experience?
- Before you accept a position, do you make sure you fully understand the position's responsibilities, conditions, and limitations (e.g., status, hours, whether the position is full-time or permanent, temporary or open-ended, policies and laws governing how you will function)?
- The terms and conditions of employment should be provided in writing (in the form of a letter or a contract from the employer) and should be fully explicated, particularly in regard to special duties that will be performed (e.g., counseling of clients with special needs).
- Anticipate receiving periodic evaluations (both oral and written) of performance.

Understanding Your Professional Responsibility

- You cannot share, delegate, or reduce the responsibility you have for your actions.
- Your primary responsibility is to the client. Resolve conflicts between your employer and your clients on the basis of this responsibility.
- Do you know and employ the performance standards, ethical principles, and practice guidelines governing the conduct of your work?

- Expect employers to neither request nor expect that you violate practice guidelines, nor should they take punitive actions should you seek to follow practice guidelines.
- Do you avoid participating in professional, research, or educational activities that violate those practice guidelines or that run counter to the promotion of human welfare?
- Do you resist pressures in your work that would violate the ethical and professional foundation of psychology?
- If you are considering undertaking classified research or professional tasks, do you recognize that such work is not subject to professional scrutiny or supervision? Thus it will be your responsibility to consider carefully the effect of that work on individuals and society and to avoid engaging in work that would otherwise be considered unethical.

Working in Special Settings

- Each setting in which you work will be governed by a particular set of procedures, laws, regulations, and practices—whether it is in local, state, or federal agencies; the criminal justice system; schools; business and industry; research facilities and programs; hospitals and health maintenance organizations; or even private practice settings. Are you sensitive to the similarities and differences between those guidelines and the ethics and practice guidelines of psychology? Do you know when those differences are appropriate and necessary?
- If you find that those differences violate ethical psychological practice, do you bring those violations to the attention of your supervisor or another authority, suggesting ways in which changes could be made that would bring them into agreement? Do you work with your employer to bring those changes into being?
- Are you aware of the varied needs of clients with whom you may be required to work in a particular setting and how the skills you have may differ from those required to meet the clients' needs?
- Are you sure that you understand the ethical implications and employer's expectations surrounding that care?
- Are you sensitive to the fact that your employer is entitled to ethical protection regarding confidentiality and other issues?
- If you become aware of unethical or illegal activity on the part of an employer and find that the employer is unwilling to change that behavior, consider carefully the effects of maintaining confidentiality. You may be ethically and legally obligated to take action to stop the employer from proceeding.

Focus 24: Providing Services in Hospitals and Other Institutions

- Are you aware of the laws regulating forms of treatment that psychologists may legally provide in hospitals and other settings?
- Do you avoid providing services in settings that do not support and enforce the ethics and practice guidelines of the profession or the laws governing practice?

• Do you know the structure and procedures of the institution so that you can provide efficient, effective service within the environment?

• Have you identified and adhered to the limitations that are placed on the services you provide by policy, by law, and by practice guidelines within the setting? Do you know the limits of your skills and will you learn how to perform the tasks assigned to you?

• Do you understand the nature of the services provided by others on staff at all levels and understand how the services that you provide support or are supported by the services that they provide? Do you demonstrate respect for others' contributions to meeting clients' needs?

• When making oral and written reports that others will use, are you accurate but brief? Do you avoid using undefined terminology that those who are not mental health professionals cannot understand?

• Are you flexible, open, helpful, and action-oriented? Remember that you are working in an environment that depends upon teamwork and upon the ability to intervene directly and often immediately to resolve a client's problems.

• Do you avoid institutional politics? You cannot ignore the hierarchy, but some actions may inhibit your ability to serve your clients effectively.

Focus 25: Documentation in Hospitals and Other Institutions

• In litigation involving hospitals, it is frequently stated that "If it's not in the chart, it didn't happen."

• Hospitals and other institutional settings, whether they provide mental health care either primarily or incidentally, frequently require a different kind and degree of documentation than might be required in many other practice settings. Typically, more information, observations, and so forth must be thoroughly documented.

• Do you know the law governing ownership of and access to client files in such settings?

• Can you correctly use any required forms?

Documentation Typically Required

• Documentation required from psychologists could include, among other items, the following:
    1. admitting notes
    2. consultation notes
    3. diagnostic reports
    4. treatment plans
    5. detailed psychological testing reports
    6. progress notes
    7. orders that are written on charts
    8. discharge summaries.

• *Admitting notes* may be prepared by one or more individuals who may constitute a formal intake and treatment team. The notes should include:

1. the client's name
2. other pertinent personal data (age, sex)
3. preliminary diagnosis
4. history of the current problem
5. treatment history
6. current medications
7. physical problems and disorders
8. mental status exams
9. instructions on how the patient should be approached by staff and others
10. any special precautions needed for certain conditions (e.g., allergies, suicidal or violent tendencies, conditions needing observation).

- *Treatment plans* provide the rules under which the client will receive treatment and, if institutionalized, will live while in the institution. The plan should anticipate the client's needs for safety and for service. A treatment plan may be required from every service unit in the setting that provides treatment to the client. Some institutions require the use of a treatment plan form. Treatment plans for psychological care could include:
  1. recommendations from other staff members about ways to approach treatment
  2. classifications related to the client's freedom to move about
  3. visitation privileges
  4. short- and long-term goals
  5. planned approaches to treatment

- *Progress notes* document all things that are done with the client and are made *immediately* by each person who interacts with the client as the actions are performed. Progress notes typically include:
  1. date and time of service
  2. length of time spent with the patient
  3. type of service (e.g., individual therapy session)
  4. name and degree or title of the person rendering service
  5. reference to the treatment plan
  6. description of what occurred and of the patient's response
  7. how that intervention affects future treatment
  8. what other staff members should do for follow-up

- *Treatment orders* are included in the progress notes and written on the client's chart if charts are used. Hospital privileges may limit the psychologist's writing of treatment orders. Treatment orders typically include:
  1. client category or status assigned in institution
  2. visitation rights and passes
  3. activities
  4. interventions (behavior management)
  5. treatment modalities
  6. medications activity (inclusion varies according to locality)

- *Discharge summaries* are formal documents that summarize the treatment that the client has received and are frequently provided to other professionals who treat the client after he or she leaves the institution. Summaries could include:

1. documentation of how the client progressed and responded through the various stages of treatment
2. procedures, tests, and medications used
3. critical incidents
4. treatment to be given subsequent to discharge, including where it will be offered and by whom
5. diagnosis on discharge (including explanation of why this may have changed since admission)

Focus 26: Being a Public Psychologist

- All "advice" given should be scientifically valid.
- Are you familiar with the guidelines provided by the pertinent boards and committees of the APA (Ethics Committee, Board of Professional Affairs, Board of Scientific Affairs) and with state and Federal Trade Commission regulations on advertising by your profession? Do you consider them carefully before engaging in public presentations about psychology or before providing advice to consumers?
- Are you sensitive to the areas of ethical vulnerability and to the possibility that information you provide to consumers may be misunderstood or misused? Do you avoid assuming that your audience will either understand or take the time to understand what you are saying?
- Do you avoid providing advice or information in an area for which you lack appropriate training or experience?
- Do you clearly state the limitations of the information you provide?
- Do you always prepare carefully for live presentations, recognizing that nervousness, the pressures of a radically different environment, the presence of an audience, and other factors can lead you to become confused or to make misstatements? Do you become familiar with the presentation or broadcast settings in advance if possible?
- During live presentations, particularly those involving questions and answers, do you take the time to think before speaking? Do you avoid becoming emotional when faced with conflict or issues about which you feel strongly?
- Do you avoid representing theory as fact or beliefs held by a few psychologists as being held by all? If a topic is controversial, are you objective? Do you provide the names of colleagues who can speak to the other side of the issue?
- Are you aware of *how* you are saying what you are saying? Do you define terms? Do you use language that the audience will understand?
- If documents or films are being produced from your presentation, do you understand the rules for editing what you say? Can you participate in the process?
- Are you sensitive to the limitations of evaluating and providing appropriate diagnoses to consumers by radio, telephone, or book? When giving instructions or advice, do you consider the implications of such advice for the individual?
- Do you screen callers and media participants in order to protect those who should not have media exposure? Develop procedures for referral to qualified professionals and trained individuals.

Invitations To Write, Speak, Provide an Interview, or Appear in Person

- Do you determine the purpose of the presentation, when and how it will be presented, and the kind of audience that will be addressed?
- Do you know who is going to sponsor or present the program or publish the work? If you know nothing about them, you should learn their affiliation and reputation before accepting. You should not accept the invitation unless you have confidence in their reliability and respectability.
- Regardless of the pressure that may be applied, you should not agree to address or speak about issues that you are not qualified to address.

Focus 27: Taking Care of Yourself (Burnout)

- If you cannot function effectively, you will be unable to meet professional and ethical responsibilities to clients and the profession.
- Are you alert to the signs of fatigue, distress, impairment, and burnout? Such signs include:
    1. increased stress at home and in the workplace
    2. irritability, emotional exhaustion, and depersonalization of others
    3. reduced personal accomplishment
    4. workaholism, isolation
    5. alcohol or substance abuse
    6. inappropriate or unusual behavior
    7. indecisiveness, procrastination, angry outbursts
    8. changes in patterns of behavior
- If you do experience distress, do you avoid assuming that you are capable of handling the situation? Do you ignore the problem out of fear of harm to your image?
- Do you and your colleagues have access to programs for the treatment of professional distress? If not, do you support their development and enhancement for the sake of yourself and your colleagues?
- Do you know how to manage stress and workload, and have you learned techniques for coping? Such training could include time management, relaxation techniques, recreational activities, and similar techniques.
- Do you take care of your personal needs? Do you monitor your health and seek medical and dental attention as needed? Do you take vacations and relax in other ways?
- Do you know how to recognize the signs and symptoms of the abuse of substances, including alcohol, prescription drugs, and over-the-counter drugs? Do you monitor your own use of alcohol and other substances?
- Do you listen to family, friends, and colleagues if they indicate you appear to be showing signs of distress? Do you seriously consider what they say and take steps to get help if their observations are accurate?
- Consider seeking the help of a colleague or a program if you find that you are exhibiting signs of distress.

- If the comments or complaints of a colleague's clients, students, or others with whom he or she interacts indicate that your colleague is in distress, do you take steps to ameliorate the problem?

See Chapter 11 in *Professionals in Distress* (VandenBos and Duthie, 1986) for a comprehensive discussion of professional distress and suggestions about actions you can take to help yourself and your colleagues.

Focus 28: Preparing for Retirement and Planning for Death or Disability

- You should plan ahead for retirement, not only to insure your own well-being but also to insure the well-being of your clients.
- Give yourself plenty of time to think through the process and your needs. The larger your practice, the longer it will take you to prepare. Allow at least 1 to 2 years and as many as 5 to 10 years to complete this process.
- Develop a network of colleagues and other professionals to whom you can refer clients who need to continue treatment.
- Consider whether you wish to curtail practice entirely or to provide some services on a part-time or consultative basis.
- If you are going to continue to offer therapy, consider which clients you will continue to treat. Why? How will some clients react if you abandon them in favor of other clients?
- Set a firm date for closing your office well in advance (perhaps 1, 2, or 3 years?).
- Develop procedures for closing down your office and for referring clients.
- Announce your decision to colleagues and employees.
- Review client files and determine who should be referred, who may be able to terminate within the time period before your retirement, and how your clients are likely to react when they learn of your retirement.
- Consider how you will announce your decision to clients and plan what you are going to say. Therapists, in particular, must allow enough time overall (perhaps as few as 6 months or as many as 12 months depending on the nature of the clients' conditions) to help clients adjust to this decision to retire.
- Consider when to stop accepting new clients and when to begin referring current clients to new therapists. Some sources suggest that you do this 3 to 6 months before retirement, depending on the nature of your practice.
- You should obtain client releases for providing their records to their new therapists. Determine how to provide those records (copies of actual files? summaries?). If possible, meet with the new therapists to discuss clients' histories.
- You should retain copies of all files.
- Do not overlook the business aspects of your practice. Review insurance policies and determine which to cancel and the nature of coverage you will need to continue. Close unnecessary bank accounts. Discontinue other services at an appropriate time before you close the office.
- Collect all fees due from clients and from those to whom you provide consultative services. It is advisable to receive payment no later than 30 days after

you close. Give clients adequate warning of this requirement. Pay all fees you owe to others.

- Arrange for secure storage of the records not being transferred.
- Develop procedures for handling inquiries after you close your practice. Inform employees, telephone answering services, colleagues, and others who may need to know of those procedures.
- Be prepared to receive inquiries for some time, even years, after retirement. Develop procedures for how you will handle them.

Death or Severe Disability

- It is best to prepare for the possibility of your death or disability while you are practicing. However, to protect both your clients and yourself, you certainly should do so as part of your retirement planning.
- Decide who could step in for you to either take over your practice, supervise its dissolution, or monitor your records. It would be most appropriate to arrange for a psychologist to perform this task. Inform your executor and appropriate family members of who should act for you.
- Prepare instructions that detail how to support clients, provide referrals, handle records, and perform other important tasks in the event that you are unable to direct the process.
- Inform staff members about what to do.
- Be sure to provide for the ethical handling of the entire process.
- If you become disabled but are still capable of doing so, review files and make referrals yourself. If possible, orient therapists to whom you refer clients.
- Arrange for the appropriate handling of records, including retention of copies, especially for inactive clients or for those whom you do not refer.
- Make sure that files are not destroyed in your absence.

Focus 29: The Psychologist as Witness

- There is an important distinction between a lay witness and an expert witness. Any citizen, including a psychologist, may be called on as a lay witness to report what he or she saw or heard as relevant to the issue before the court (e.g., a witness to an accident). An expert witness is called upon to render an expert opinion that may go far beyond the facts of a case (e.g., to testify as to what the mental status of the defendant may have been at the time of the crime).
- In serving as an expert witness, regardless of how you came to be a witness or whose witness you are, your function is to provide an unbiased, straightforward evaluation of a situation or individual and to provide a professional opinion that can be significant in deciding the outcome of the case.
- If you are not familiar with how the court system works, what a courtroom looks like, trial procedures, how you will be questioned, and so forth, you should educate yourself. You could ask the party you are serving for orientation, ask an

attorney colleague for help, or visit the court during a case in which a colleague is testifying.

- If you do not understand the rules of evidence in the court in which the case will be heard (e.g., What constitutes hearsay evidence?) and what determines the legitimacy of a specific plea (e.g., not guilty by reason of insanity), learn them. What you as a psychologist may consider pertinent may not be pertinent under the law.

- Do you know the legal meaning of important terms, for example, *mental illness, competency, fitness,* and *insanity*? Remember, these terms may be defined differently in different jurisdictions.

- Do you avoid allowing your attitudes toward the issues of the case (e.g., nature of the crime, foundation of the suit, the validity of the law or need for system reform) or the individuals involved (e.g., personal belief in a client's guilt or innocence, attitude toward a child committing a parent) to alter the manner in which you approach your assigned task?

- If you do not believe that you are qualified to serve as an expert witness or find that you are unable to maintain your objectivity, do you refuse to accept the case?

- Do you understand the grounds under which you may be excused from serving or may refuse to serve? (For example, can you refuse a court-ordered appointment? If you do not believe there is sufficient time to perform the task required in a professional way, can you obtain additional time or refuse?) You should request release immediately if you feel it is necessary.

- Be aware that, although you have prepared an evaluation, there is no legal requirement that the individual requesting it has to use it unless it is a court-ordered evaluation. It may not be used at all, particularly if some aspect of it does not support the case being presented by the parties who requested the evaluation.

- A colleague or another expert may provide information that refutes your testimony, and you may not have an opportunity to respond. Assuming that your colleague (and you) have adhered to the ethics and guidelines of your professions in deriving your opinions, remember that such differences represent a professional disagreement, not a personal attack.

Understanding the Role You Will Play in Court

- Will you be retained by the plaintiff or the defendant, act as a friend of the court (*amicus curiae*), or be a court-appointed participant? How do your qualifications make you suitable for that role?

- Avoid confusing your role as an evaluator with that of a therapist. Avoid attempting to treat an individual for whom you are performing a court-ordered evaluation, if possible. You should recommend treatment if you feel the person requires it.

- Obtain the following basic information when contacted to serve:
    1. name, address, and telephone number of the individual who contacted you and of the attorney with whom you will deal

2. whether you will be required to respond to a request for documents, to provide written responses to interrogatories (written questions), to attend and testify at a deposition, or to attend and testify in court
3. the issues you will be asked to address
4. the expected date of trial
5. time and place where it will be held
6. name of the judge
7. type of court (e.g., local, state, federal)

- Do not overlook business aspects of the arrangements: Establish a fee or schedule of payment, obtain a letter of commitment, set up the first appointment, and so forth.

- Be sure to determine who is responsible for payment—the party being evaluated or the attorney representing that party. It may be helpful if the payment plan is put in the form of a letter or contract.

- It is always wise to collect any fees prior to presentation of the results. Prepayment avoids the problem of payment refusal if the client does not like the results, and it aids in assuring an independent evaluation.

- Obtain a full description of the facts of the case and the issues that make it necessary for you to perform an evaluation of the individual or to develop an opinion regarding why a specific event occurred or what its effects may or may not have been.

- If you are to evaluate a particular individual, find out when he or she is available for examination and where examinations can take place (e.g., Is he or she confined? Can the person come to your office? Must the examination be conducted in a jail?). Request records that you believe will be useful (e.g., personal history, military record, records of previous mental health treatment).

Informing the Individual Being Evaluated

- Know the statutory limits protecting confidentiality.
- Do you always determine whether the individual being evaluated understands why he or she is being evaluated and how the results of that evaluation will be used? If you are performing a court-ordered evaluation, does the individual understand that you are acting on behalf of the court?

- Do you inform the individual of his or her rights under the law regarding the evaluation and of limitations on confidentiality? If possible, obtain a signed acknowledgment that you did so. Such an acknowledgment should include the dates of examination and testing, a statement of the circumstances under which they were performed (e.g., court-ordered, requested by whom and for what purpose), how the results will be used and by whom, and signatures of you or the examiner, the individual being examined, and a witness, if needed.

- If the client is a defendant in a criminal case, keep in mind that there are constitutional limits to disclosure, such as, Fifth Amendment protection against self-incrimination. It is vital to include a statement in the signed acknowledgment that the results of the tests and examination may be used against him or her.

- If the individual could benefit from therapy, it may be appropriate to offer to provide a referral or to treat the individual; however, do not attempt to practice therapy while performing the evaluation.

Issues in Performing Evaluations

- Do you select tests with care, being sure that you understand both their limitations and their usefulness *in terms of the goal of the evaluation*? Be sensitive to special characteristics of the individual being evaluated, such as ethnic, cultural, language, and age issues.
- *Competency to stand trial is a legal, not a psychological, issue.* Do you know the legal definition of the term? Typically, such an evaluation is requested by a defendant's attorney. Do you always determine whether the defendant understands the charges against him or her, the implications of the plea to be entered and the results of the verdict, the court procedures and participants' roles, and how he or she should behave in the courtroom? The defendant's intellectual capacity and neuropsychological factors should be considered.
- *Plea of insanity is a legal, not a psychological, issue.* Do you know the legal definition of the term? Do you know the insanity test (M'Naghten, American Law Institute Model Code, other?) used in the trial jurisdiction, upon whom the burden of proof lies, and what constitutes adequate proof? Typically, you should examine the events of the crime thoroughly, learn what the defendant recalls, talk to witnesses, perform all necessary and appropriate psychological evaluations of the individual, obtain a thorough history (of the individual and his or her family, including medical and psychological history), assess reading skills (e.g., Can he or she read? Can he or she read English?), and form an opinion regarding the reality of the individual's claim (i.e., is the individual faking?).
- *Custody of a minor child.* Do you understand the background of the case, including issues surrounding potential child abuse? Evaluations should be conducted in private, without a third party being present. Consider the history of the case and the background on family relations prior to filing for divorce and since filing. When evaluating a child, evaluate the child's personal history (e.g., school performance, behavior patterns to date), intellectual and psychological status, and the child's attitudes as well as pertinent psychological factors. Consider evaluating all concerned family members and others with whom the child interacts. Is this possible? What steps should you take to do this? When evaluating an adult regarding suitability for custody or contact with the child, do a thorough standard psychological evaluation. In the absence of supporting evidence or research, avoid predicting how a parent will behave.
- Never rely on testing the child as the only means of making recommendations regarding custody. A thorough evaluation of all significant parties is necessary.
- Performing custody evaluations is a high-risk area for malpractice litigation because the stakes are always high, and someone always loses. A parent who is not awarded custody, loses visitation rights, or has visitation rights restricted may file a malpractice suit against the psychologist because challenging his or her evaluation may appear to be the only way to challenge the court's decision.

• In providing other evaluations for use in the court, be clear about the factors that are pertinent to the case and avoid introducing extraneous elements. In some instances (e.g., personal injury cases), it may be appropriate to provide a prediction of how an individual will react or behave, but base such predictions on research, or qualify your opinion by explaining why you believe it to be valid.

Preparing Written Reports

• Even if portions of your activity are reported orally, do you prepare a complete written report providing all information you have derived, unless specifically requested not to do so by an attorney who has retained your services to evaluate his or her case?
  • Such reports may include:
    1. name, age, and pertinent data such as educational level and reading ability of person evaluated, if tests required the client to read
    2. a statement of the reason for referral (and who referred the individual)
    3. a summary of background factors that are pertinent to the psychological evaluation (e.g., individual's psychological and pertinent medical history, summary of records examined and their sources, summary of interviews with others)
    4. the process used in the evaluation (e.g., tests used and how they were administered, number of interviews)
    5. a succinct summary of research findings pertinent to your findings, recommendations, or predictions
• If the individual you interview should have therapy or another form of treatment (e.g., medical treatment), you may make specific recommendations and provide a list of areas of concern.
• Be aware of research that may contradict your findings and be prepared to defend your results.
• Retain copies of all materials you provide as part of your evaluation.

Depositions

• A *deposition* is a form of written testimony given by a witness under oath. It has the same standing as sworn testimony given in a court.
• Typically, the witness (called the *deposee*) gives the statement in the presence of a lawyer or another officer of the court. The statement is taken down by a stenographer or recorded on tape and is then later transcribed in written form. This written statement is then signed by the witness.
• Depositions can be presented as evidence in court, and the witness need not be present at that time, although he or she may be asked to be present.
• Technically, depositions are subject to question; that is, the opposing side in the case may present either their own depositions in rebuttal or may place witnesses on the stand to rebut testimony provided in a deposition. If the witness who gave the testimony is present in the court, the witness may be called to the stand to further explain statements made in the deposition.

• If you are asked to provide a deposition (either with or without being under subpoena), you should ask yourself the same questions you would ask whenever you give testimony (see the preceding sections in this Focus list). You should also prepare for a deposition in the same way that you prepare for testimony in court, making sure that your files are organized and you are able to respond appropriately to questions you might be asked. Consult a lawyer if you feel it is necessary.

• Once you have given your deposition and have received a copy for your signature, read the written statement carefully. If you note errors that you may have inadvertently made or errors that were introduced during transcription, you may either (a) provide additional information orally and have that added to the statement or (b) annotate the statement by hand. Regardless of how the errors are introduced, do not sign a deposition if it does not accurately reflect your testimony. And remember that the statement is given under oath; deliberate deception constitutes a form of perjury.

Preparations for Testifying

• Prepare carefully by reviewing with your attorney your case file, written report, and other pertinent material. It may be useful to prepare a set of notes detailing relevant research to which you can refer during testimony (e.g., statistics about prevalence or reliability) should additional questions be asked. Be aware that such notes may be subject to cross-examination.

• You will be required to state your qualifications, including length of experience and specific experience in areas of concern to the case.

• Prepare any support materials you plan to use (e.g., charts, graphs, example cases) in advance of the trial.

• When testifying, stay calm. Think before answering a question. Do not allow the attorneys to pressure you into making statements that do not represent your opinion regarding the matter at hand. Should it become necessary, ask for permission from the judge to provide additional information.

Focus 30: Handling Complaints About Your Performance or Ethics

• All clients have a right to complain (to you, to your supervisor, to a professional body), whether or not their complaints are well founded.

• If a client registers a complaint during a session or in the office, consider it carefully. Does it represent actual dissatisfaction with your performance or does it reflect a problem that is being or should be considered in therapy?

• Decide how to adjust your handling of the case under the circumstances. If appropriate, discuss with the client why he or she made the complaint, what it represents in therapy, how the client views it, and how you feel about it.

• Document all complaints, regardless of their origin or foundation. Note the date, the name of the person complaining, the nature of the complaint, your response, and the outcome of your discussion with the client. Even minor complaints should be noted because patterns of complaining may develop or the complaints may escalate beyond your ability to control them. Documentation should be part of the client's file, but you may also wish to maintain a separate file of all complaints received.

Formal Complaints

• A formal complaint registered with a professional board or organization may or may not be pertinent under the law, but the verdict in a court action, particularly in a criminal case, may be directly pertinent to the actions taken by a professional board or organization. In some states, criminal conviction is automatically grounds for denial or revocation of a license to practice. However, formal censure by a state professional board in a matter of ethics may be subject to review by a national organization's ethics committee before formal action on a national level is taken.

• Familiarize yourself with the formal complaint processes for the licensing agency or professional board governing your practice and for state and national associations of which you are a member. Obtain copies of relevant procedures and know your rights under those procedures. A statute of limitations for filing complaints may be in place.

• The APA Ethics Committee has jurisdiction only over members, fellows, and associates of the American Psychological Association, although it may choose to provide an opinion regarding the actions of a nonmember in order to protect the public. If you are a member of the APA, become thoroughly familiar with the procedures of the Ethics Committee.

• Your employer should have formal procedures for handling complaints. If not, recommend that procedures be developed.

• Ignorance, carelessness, or misinformation on the part of the individual bringing the complaint are not always grounds for the dismissal of such complaints.

• If a client makes a formal complaint, do not take it lightly. Take steps to prepare for answering the complaint.

• If the client who has filed a formal complaint is still a client and wishes to continue therapy, obtain advice from an experienced colleague, your supervisor, or (if necessary) a lawyer regarding the suitability of continuing therapy. Discuss the situation with the client. Provide a referral if appropriate.

• Procedures may vary, but it is likely that you will be asked to provide a formal response to the complaint and copies of pertinent documents. Be prepared to protect yourself and to provide this information, but remember that you must maintain the client's right to confidentiality at all times and under all circumstances. Information that is not pertinent to the complaint should be protected.

• In some states and under certain conditions, however, the client's right to confidentiality may be waived if a client places his or her mental status at issue or brings a malpractice suit against the practitioner. This should be considered in relation to information you provide.

• Be truthful in responding to all queries and appear before the body receiving the complaint if you are requested to do so.

• Do not assume that you can handle the formalities without legal advice. Obtain legal counsel if necessary.

- Regardless of the outcome or whether the complaint is carried through to the end of the process, be sensitive to the effect on the therapeutic relationship. Terminating therapy may be your only wise alternative.

Focus 31: What To Do if You Are Sued

- Whether you consider the grounds for a lawsuit brought against you to be factual or to be the product of a client acting out in an effort to punish you or control you, you must treat the suit seriously.
- If a suit has been filed against you, do not attempt to work it out by contacting the client or conducting more therapy. Anything that you do at that point may be used against you in the litigation. Once a suit is filed, your relationship with the client is supplanted by a relationship with the client's attorney, who is not interested in "therapeutically" working out the problem with you.
- Do not attempt personally to resolve or settle the case with the client or with the plaintiff's attorney.
- Familiarize yourself thoroughly with your liability policy when you obtain it. Do not wait until you are sued. Know the limits of coverage, the company's procedures regarding when the company will begin to act or provide you with a lawyer, and similar procedures.
- Notify your insurance agent and company immediately if a client threatens a suit or if you receive a subpoena notifying you of such a suit.
- Know whether you are free to select a lawyer or must accept the lawyer selected by the insurance company. If you do not like the lawyer, are you free to request another?
- If you are uncomfortable with the legal counsel provided by the insurance carrier and it cannot be changed, consider the advisability of using a lawyer of your own to provide advice or act directly on your behalf in cooperation with the insurance company's attorney.
- Be prepared for the case to take a considerable length of time, perhaps even years.
- Do not destroy or otherwise alter files or reports pertinent to the client's case.
- When the plaintiff, plaintiff's attorney, or the court requests documents, do not provide documents or other information directly. Provide them only with the advice of, and through, your attorney, and provide only what is requested. Always retain the originals of documents; provide copies only.
- Do not disclose information that will violate the client's right to confidentiality unless the law governing the case being brought limits the client's right to confidentiality (e.g., if the client's sanity is pertinent to the charges, your record of evaluation of the client's sanity is pertinent). Do not provide information that is not pertinent to the case. Always follow the advice of competent legal counsel. Be sure to protect yourself.
- Prepare summaries of events related to the case for your own use and the use of your attorney.

- Professional case consultation with colleagues is not generally considered privileged information.
- Do not make self-incriminating statements to staff, to the client, or to the client's lawyers. Do not discuss the case with anyone, including your own family, other than your attorney.
- Refer all communications with the plaintiff or plaintiff's attorney to your attorney.
- Do not continue to treat a client who is suing you.

5 ———————————————————————

The Practical Side of Professional Liability: Insurance

As a psychologist, you may be as exemplary as Caesar's wife—avoiding even the appearance of wrongdoing—and still get sued. However, there is still much you can do to minimize that likelihood and even to avoid a malpractice suit. The principle of self-care is inherent in being a well-prepared, functioning practitioner. Taking care of one's own mental and physical well-being is necessary if one is to practice effectively and efficiently. Many psychologists believe that their personal security— including both their reputation and their financial resources—must be protected. Thus, they believe that there is only one thing they can do to really protect themselves: Buy insurance, specifically, professional liability insurance (PLI).

In the introduction to this volume, we emphasized that the book's purpose is not to sell a particular vendor's PLI or to further complicate the practitioner's life. At the same time, because we strongly believe that litigation is a reality one must be prepared to face, we wish to encourage each practitioner to at least consider purchasing PLI—but to do so with a clear understanding of what PLI is (and is not). Thus, this chapter is intended to provide some basic information about PLI.

The word *liability* not only encompasses the theory of accountability used in tort law but also has another, more concrete meaning: It means legal damages, money you could be required to pay to compensate a plaintiff who can prove a malpractice case.

If you are like most practitioners, every month or quarter you get a reminder in the mail about various types of insurance, and your checkbook register shows that you paid the premiums. But do you really know what insurance is and how it works? Do you believe that you need it? Few practitioners reading this book would go without health and automobile insurance. Surprisingly, however, a number of practitioners seriously consider practicing psychology without insuring themselves against a malpractice claim. There are three common rationales behind this reasoning, which we will discuss presently. But first, there is a basic question that should be answered.

Who Needs PLI?

Who needs PLI? Anyone who might be sued. A better way to say this is "any practitioner who undertakes a duty of care." Most policies are designed to cover those who actually deliver clinical services. But psychologists who work as industrial or organizational consultants or academic or research psychologists, even those whose only nonacademic professional activity is limited to research, testing, or evaluation, may want or need coverage. Remember that subjects participating in research projects can and do experience loss and harm consequent to these procedures. Employee screening programs developed by a psychologist may fail in practice. And the practitioner accused of negligence in an evaluation may have to defend the test instrument itself, its relevance, its proper application, and his or her interpretation.

Almost no professional psychologist does not interact with people as clients or subjects in the course of his or her work. Thus, a working hypothesis is that everyone needs some form of protection. (The notable exception to this is psychologists who work in government departments that enjoy legal immunity from suit.)

A great many professionals come under the protective umbrella of an employer such as a clinic, hospital, university, government department, or even a fellow practitioner at the head of a group practice—and falsely believe themselves immune from personal liability. Practitioners working for or within an institution who believe they are adequately covered by the institution would be well advised to inquire more closely.

Are you covered when your work takes you off-site? What about delivering services to those who are not clients of your employer? Even if the delivery of services is covered by your employer's policy, are you covered as *an individual*? Probably not, unless you are actually named as an *additional insured* on the policy. Moreover, in these and other circumstances, it is unlikely that the attorney representing your employer's insurance carrier will hold your personal interests over those of the institution should a conflict arise. In the worst case, they might even argue that you personally rather than the institution were liable.

If you are involved in any sort of collegial relationship—as a supervisor, cotherapist, or even office-mate—ask your carrier about any liability you might incur for the acts of these people. Lawsuits have been brought against therapists who have had no professional connection at all with others sharing their office space. In such situations, the plaintiff's attorney will name each person occupying the premises on the theory that a conspiracy may exist between the parties involved. Protecting yourself against such situations may be a simple matter, but the issue is one that needs to be raised with your carrier before it is tested by a litigious plaintiff using the "shotgun approach." Subject to underwriting approval, many policies permit the listing of additional insured parties for an extra premium payment.

Many practitioners need to extend their PLI to cover a corporation or people working with and for them. Insurance carriers are generally open to discussing such coverage, but separate insurance for the corporation is probably necessary. It is also common for PLI to automatically cover all nonprofessional (clerical, administrative, etc.) employees for no increase in premium, because they are not directly subject to a malpractice claim. But you must inquire specifically about this and obtain a written statement about the policy coverage from your carrier.

Unlicensed practitioners whose duties are professional, including psychometrists, cotherapists, counselors, and other nonlicensed persons providing services, are also subject to malpractice laws. They can usually be included on your policy, but their level of education and training as well as the services they provide (factors that might be cited to make them viable targets for a malpractice suit) will be considered in determining how much additional premium payment is required.

When a single policy covers a partnership of several psychologists, each practitioner needs to be certain that he or she is named as an additional insured and to be aware that each member of the partnership is liable for the individual acts of the other members.

Why Do *You* Need PLI?

You need PLI for two reasons. First, you could be sued for malpractice. If you lose that suit, you could be assessed damages for thousands, even hundreds of thousands of dollars. Your property could be taken and your future wages or income could be attached. Second, even if the threat of a lawsuit is not well founded, even if you are innocent of any wrongdoing or negligence, a lawsuit filed against you cannot be ignored. The legal machinery has been set in motion. To stop it, you will need to take legal countermeasures of some kind. The legal expenses of even a frivolous suit can exceed several thousand dollars. In many situations, the legal expenses exceed any damages awarded.

Once a suit has been filed, there are typically three legal options:
1. The lawyers of the defendant and plaintiff may reach an agreement that results in the suit being dropped with no liability incurred.
2. The suit may be pursued in court.
3. The suit may be settled.

In an ideal world, lawsuits would be brought only by those who have good cause to believe they have been harmed and see no other recourse for being compensated. Lawsuits would be brought only against practitioners who have failed in their duty of care. As an ethical, competent psychologist, you would never have to face a lawsuit.

In the real world, however, even the innocent are sued. From the moment the suit is brought, the defendant psychologist begins to accumulate legal expenses, faces potential damage to his or her reputation, loses time from work, and undergoes enormous stress. In collaboration with legal counsel, the psychologist will consider whether there is legally accepted proof of the psychologist's innocence. Thus, as is true with much civil litigation, the defendants and their insurance companies often choose not to struggle openly in court and, instead, reach an agreement with the plaintiff to drop the claim—on the theory that the cure (being adjudged not guilty) might be worse (too costly in money, time, and damaged reputations) than the disease.

If a defendant psychologist is considering such an option, it should not be done without a great deal of thought. Such agreements typically mean paying the client a portion of the amount named in the suit. The insurance industry views settlements as part of the cost of doing business because of the high cost of defending even weak malpractice suits and the risk of large jury awards. Properly negotiated settlements may, in fact, help reduce the cost of PLI for the specific carrier and the overall profession. It is around the issue of settlement that an individual psychologist is most likely to wonder whether his or her interests and those of the carrier are the same.

Professional psychology can and does play a part in ameliorating one of the imperfections in the system—frivolous suits. In some states, review boards of law and mental health experts have been established to screen malpractice cases before they can proceed to the trial stage. The goal is to discourage frivolous litigation and suits brought purely for monetary gain, and to better allocate society's resources by letting only those claims with a sound basis and a good possibility of prevailing proceed to trial. This type of filtering process may play a part in reducing the number of malpractice cases.

At the same time, such review boards have been criticized because they may reduce access to the court system by those who cannot afford necessary legal counsel to represent their claims at the review level. It must always be remembered, however, that inherent in such panels' actions is the duty of care. If the panel's judgment favors a plaintiff, it is likely that there is at least a question of wrongdoing. This apparent endorsement of the plaintiff's claim can be discouraging for even an innocent psychologist and can affect his or her decisions about how to proceed with a defense.

Are There Valid Reasons Not To Carry PLI?

The need to carry PLI is usually questioned on the basis of one of three rationales: (a) Only the guilty get sued; (b) the chances of being sued or of having to pay out more money than one has are minuscule; and (c) liability insurance only serves to attract suits. However, you should thoroughly examine these rationales before you make a decision.

The First Rationale: Malpractice suits happen to careless people who may not be guilty of negligence but are probably guilty of something.

Some psychologists believe that honesty, honor, good intentions, and their interpersonal skills will shield them from possible lawsuits. They are like careful drivers who drive without insurance because they believe that their conscientiousness will protect them from accidents, at least until, as they sit at a red light, a pedestrian stumbles into their car, breaks an arm, and brings a lawsuit against them for ten million dollars. As psychologists, these careful practitioners may one day open the door and be handed a subpoena to answer charges of sexual misconduct (or failure to treat correctly, etc.) made by one of their current or former clients. Unfortunately, complaints and charges can be filed even when a practitioner is not professionally negligent.

The Second Rationale: Why should I buy insurance for malpractice when my chances of being sued for a substantial sum are so small? I would be better off putting the premium into my own reserve fund. It would probably cover my costs if I am sued.

Some practitioners do not think that the degree of their own potential liability, that is, their chances of being sued and the potential cost of dealing with the problem, warrants the cost of insurance. They do a personal cost–benefit analysis, and they decide to "go bare" (i.e., to forgo professional liability insurance).

To give this rationale the benefit of the doubt, let's examine for the moment what the statistics tell us. As a practicing psychologist, how likely are you to be sued? And what are the likely award amounts involved? An analysis of the data gleaned from a large group of insured psychologists provides some answers.

A Look at the Experience of Psychologists Insured Through the PLI Program Endorsed by the APAIT

Frequency of Claims Filed

How likely are you to be sued as a practicing psychologist? Ideally, to answer this question, all those who practice psychology, regardless of their group affiliation or insurance status, should be polled over a statistically valid period. To date, this has not been done. There are good data, however, for a very substantial subgroup, the 36,000 practitioners currently insured under the Professional Liability Program sponsored by the American Psychological Association Insurance Trust (APAIT) since 1976. Although conclusions drawn from this data do not include the experience of noninsured psychologists, the data have some significance.

Through February 1989, 1,416 liability claims had been filed against the program endorsed by the APAIT. An average of 125 claims are reported each year. The chance of being sued, therefore, is less than half of 1% (0.0038), or about 1 in 260 in a given year.

Average Cost per Claim

The insurance plan sponsored by the APAIT does not provide much variability in the limits of coverage and deductibles that are available. Past actuarial data do not really justify tailoring coverage to age, sex, location, or type of practice. Coverage is offered up to $1 million per claim and up to $3 million on an aggregate basis.[1] The policyholder decides how much coverage to buy.

---

[1] *Aggregate* refers to the number of suits that will be defended in one year. A $3-million aggregate means the psychologist is protected for three $1-million suits per year.

Costs include legal fees, expenses such as telephone calls and photocopying, expert witness fees, and transcript fees, as well as court costs and final monetary judgments. Thus, probable cost is difficult to determine. Many of the cases that have been reported to the APAIT are still open, that is, litigation is still pending, and thus their cost continues to mount. The amounts paid out in closed cases, that is, those suits that have been tried or settled, reflect both legal expenses and any settlements or damages awarded.

The total projected cost of each suit filed is approximately $20,000. Few practitioners have $20,000 that they can afford to risk losing in a malpractice suit, much less the million dollars or more that an award theoretically can be. If you put $450 a year into the bank at compound interest as self-protection, it will take almost 30 years—a significant portion of any professional's career—to save enough money to pay even the average cost of a case.

Although the odds are against being sued, PLI will guard you against the potential catastrophic loss associated with a malpractice suit. The purchase of PLI is similar to the purchase of an automobile or a homeowners insurance policy. The odds are that you will never file a claim under the liability section of those policies, but you purchase coverage to guard against potential catastrophic loss.

Thus, the APAIT data suggest that the chances of being sued are small, but the costs associated with a potential suit can be high, especially in comparison with the cost of protection.

The Third Rationale: Liability insurance will attract a lawsuit like nectar attracts bees. Litigious clients and unscrupulous lawyers will use me to get at the financial resources of the insurance company.

To some degree, the entire community of mental health providers goes on trial when the difficulties of any member of that community move into the courtroom. Consider what happens if an uninsured practitioner is sued and is then unable to contain the fallout from what appears to be a personal matter. This issue is at the heart of the third argument given for going without PLI.

There are many ways to protect business and personal assets against what may happen if one is sued. Many psychologists incorporate their practices on the assumption that incorporation will protect them, but incorporation does not necessarily offer good protection from liability. Practitioners may affiliate themselves with a group that maintains insurance to protect the corporate entity. A married psychologist may vest most of his or her assets in a spouse's name. Are these defenses an alternative to PLI? Perhaps. But state law varies, and once a judgment is recorded against you, it can drain any future earnings and perhaps even existing assets, regardless of their nature.

A malpractice suit puts a practitioner's actions under close scrutiny, and the conduct and results of such a suit (victory or defeat) have an effect on many people. The availability of resources, both monetary and psychological, is often a determining factor in how well the psychologist, his or her practice, and the profession weather a suit. If you have a question about whether to carry insurance because you fear that it will lead to suits you might otherwise be spared, you might examine the responsibility you have toward:

1. *Your clients.* If you must devote your time, energy, and money to your own legal defense, it is very possible that your clients will suffer. Perhaps you will even be forced to stop working because of stress and financial difficulties.

2. *Your colleagues.* It is doubtful that potential litigants will drop their suits once they discover that suing you will not provide access to the resources of a large insurance company. There are many motives for lawsuits beyond the lure of a monetary judgment. Also, your comparative lack of resources might induce the defendant and his or her attorney to broaden their claim and try to include as codefendants others who are insured.

   If you have consulted with a colleague about a case, have referred the plaintiff for testing to another colleague, have relied on a standardized tool for an evaluation, or have shared office space with another practitioner, each source of consultation could be vulnerable to suit. This "shotgun" approach to civil litigation is a common tactic. Even if such broad efforts fail, legal and emotional costs will be exacted from those practitioners who are insured.

3. *Yourself.* Remember that, even if a suit never reaches a court or the court does not decide against the psychologist, substantial legal expenses can nonetheless be incurred. If you are uninsured, you will have to pay these costs, and you will face the suit without the benefit and experience of the carrier's specialized legal help.

Finally, the most compelling repudiation to the concept of going bare is this: The average practitioner is not clairvoyant. No matter what rationale is developed to justify the strategy of self-protection, it will suffer from the practitioner's inability to see into the future. It not possible to be definitive about what kind of protection will be needed in years hence anymore than it is possible to predict how standards of care will change and what legal precedents will be established in years to come. Keep in mind that the average claim is not reported for several years. Some suits are filed 10 years or more after the alleged events occurred! Establishing and maintaining a PLI policy offers you protection throughout your career.

Thus there is a simple answer to the question, Why should I buy PLI? You might be sued for negligence.

The more comprehensive answer is wrapped up in how the law shapes and systematizes a malpractice complaint brought against a practitioner. Being innocent or right or only human is not protection against a suit or its consequences. Professional liability insurance is the best protection against the legal and monetary consequences of such a suit.

When Should You Be Covered?

The answer to this question is not as straightforward as it may at first seem. You buy your PLI to cover the duties that could be cited in a malpractice claim. But in a surprisingly large number of cases, many months or years intervene between the occurrence of the alleged events cited in the case and the filing of the actual claim. The average time lapse between the event and the claim report is 2 to 3 years. Some suits are brought 10 years or more after the events on which they are based. The question of malpractice, however, brings into consideration questions that echo throughout one's career. You need to purchase protection not only for the policy period but also for whenever a claim might be filed. Thus, switching carriers and policy types can create a gap in protection because a policy is not in effect at the time the alleged negligence takes place or because a previous carrier is no longer required to offer protection. For this and other reasons, practitioners prefer to set up a system of insurance that will stay in place for the foreseeable future.

What About Statutes of Limitations?

Is there no time limit to the need for coverage? Yes, in fact there are statutes of limitations in state law that preclude negligence claims being filed after specified periods of time following the alleged instance of malpractice. The actual time periods, and the conditions that define them, vary from state to state. In all states, however, a suit cannot be brought under the following conditions (that is, the statute is nullified): (a) if the negligent act stopped (has not been ongoing) and has not led to other events in the chain of proximate cause that have themselves continued in time and (b) if the complainant was competent to sue during the prescribed period of the limitation and chose not to do so.

What About Competency?

Competency is a subject not easily reduced to a formula. Practitioners who are called to testify on the question will often find themselves embroiled in a complex legal and psychological debate. Rules of general competency that develop in case law and tend to be applied routinely in a court can be combatted by evidence about whether the client was in fact competent to perform a specific act. Thus, even if your own evaluation of a client takes his or her competency for granted, such a person could bring a malpractice claim years after the statute of limitations had presumably expired. The question of competency to sue during the prescribed period then would become a subject of legal dispute, with the plaintiff's attorney free to develop "new" evidence and to bring in other experts on the question.

Once the psychological debate is joined, the question of a plaintiff's competency can be extended far beyond whether he or she is mentally retarded or organically impaired, conditions to which the term *competency* is most often applied. And attorneys may have little difficulty developing evidence to indicate that plaintiffs fail the general tests of competence most often applied by the courts, which require the individual to be aware of the facts and to understand the issues of their situation, to have sufficient self-awareness to understand the significance of that situation and their own mental condition, and to be able to demonstrate an ability to act on this awareness.

Determining competency to sue and, therefore, the start of the time period specified in the statute of limitations, is further complicated when minors are involved. Most minors are not deemed legally competent until they reach the age of majority established by law in their state of residence, although this rule of law can be modified by a finding that a child has competency to perform a particular act. But practitioners treating or evaluating minors should realize that the prescribed period during which the minor can bring suit does not begin until the minor reaches the age of majority.

Thus, you cannot say with certainty whether a complaint brought many years after the alleged negligence will be excluded because of the statute of limitations in state law. You therefore need insurance that will cover you for the periods when you were actually performing duties that could be cited in a lawsuit as negligent and could thereby provide a cause of action.

What Kinds of Policies Are Available?

Professional liability coverage is provided under two very different forms of policies: *claims-made* policies and *occurrence-based* policies.

Claims-Made Policies

A claims-made policy protects you against a claim only if you were insured at the time the alleged act occurred and you have been *continuously insured with that same carrier* up to the time the claim is filed. Under this kind of coverage, you are locked in to that carrier's claims-made policy year after year. Once you stop renewing your annual policy, even if you have retired from practice, any subsequent claims will not be covered, regardless of when the alleged act of malpractice occurred. Claims-made policies are usually less expensive, especially in the early years of coverage. Any changes in the nature of your practice (and your risk) and changes you make in your coverage under the same policy will not apply if a claim is made for an event that occurred before the change in policy coverage was made, although the original terms will apply.

If you are insured under an employer's claims-made policy, you are in effect tied to that employer forever, even if you stop working for the employer. If you have chosen a claims-made policy, it may be necessary to purchase a special kind of coverage to protect you after you retire, stop working, change jobs, or change insurance carriers. The cost of this special coverage—referred to as *tails*, *riders*, or *reporting endorsements*—could offset any savings achieved when you chose the claims-made policy. You buy the tail to cover a particular period of time, usually subsequent to your claims-made policy. Companies may offer tails for between 1 and 5 years or even longer, but the longer the period of coverage under the rider, the greater the expense. Your chances of having a belated suit brought against you do begin to decline after several years, but APAIT data (which covers 12 years) indicate that you are never impervious to a claim unless you are protected by the statute of limitations.

Occurrence-Based Policies

Occurrence-based PLI protects you against any claims that may be filed for acts that occurred during the policy period covered by the premiums you paid—even if you are no longer insured by that policy or by the insurance carrier who provided it. This sort of coverage is purchased on an annual term and is generally more expensive than claims-made policies.[2] If your coverage for that year was adequate to cover the amount of damages and costs of the suit, then any subsequent changes, in either your insurance or your circumstances, will not alter the amount of coverage that applies. In other words, you are protected forever. While most insurance carriers offer this type of permanent protection, many carriers are attempting to switch to claims-made coverage.

It is clear that the issue of malpractice brings into consideration questions that echo throughout one's career. You need to purchase protection not only for the policy period but also for whenever a claim might be filed. Thus, switching carriers and policy types could create a window of liability through which one is left unprotected, either because a policy was not in effect at the time the alleged negligence took place or because a previous carrier is no longer required to offer protection. Therefore, many practitioners prefer to set up a system of insurance that will stay in place for the foreseeable future.

How Much Insurance Should You Buy?

Most plans offer a range of coverage limits, but unlike automobile and homeowners insurance, very few PLI policies have deductibles. When considering coverage limits and deductibles, you should ask several important questions:

- How much basic coverage do you want to purchase?
- Recognizing that your policy has a coverage limit that applies to one claim only per year, how much aggregate coverage should you purchase for additional claims?
- Do the legal and defense fees expended count toward your policy limit, or are they covered for any amount? That is, are they treated as separate costs, and is there a limit on the amount of legal expenses covered or the number of cases for which legal expenses will be covered?

Policy Limits

Litigation can be contagious, and although they are not common, situations can arise in which more than one plaintiff may file a claim against you for a single incident. Insurance carriers offer a standard policy that sets one limit for a single claim and a second limit for all claims in that year. Thus, it is common to see your

---

[2]As claims-made programs mature, however, they begin to mimic occurrence programs, and the premiums for claims-made policies become as expensive as (if not more expensive than) the occurrence policies.

coverage written as "$1 million/$1 million" or "$1 million/$3 million"—the number following the slash refers to the aggregate limit for more than one claim.

In a majority of cases brought against psychologists, settlements are reached, or the defendant actually prevails at the trial. Significant legal costs are expended, however, even on these victories. Your policy may stipulate that legal costs are covered inside the per-claim limit. Without adequate aggregate coverage, however, not even legal costs will be covered for any additional claims brought during that policy year. Many psychologists will find that the hospitals and institutions in which they work will require PLI coverage of "$1 million/$3 million," that is, they will require higher aggregate.

How much is needed? That depends on whether you want protection against an average or a catastrophic claim. Most people buy insurance expecting to be fully protected from any legal costs and damages. It appears from APAIT data that coverage in the low six figures might be sufficient. Is buying lower coverage on the chance that a suit will not be a large-award case worth the risk? With the APAIT-endorsed policy, the premium for minimum coverage available in 1990 is $459, and this protects you for the costs of a single claim up to a limit of $100,000. For nearly a 50% higher premium, you can purchase the $1 million maximum, or 10 times the coverage, making this extra expenditure 10 times more effective buying protection. This is true for most, if not all, carriers. So once you have decided to buy PLI, you will see that buying more of it is a bargain. You should keep in mind that if you are buying occurrence-based PLI, your policy limit for a given year will be in effect even if a claim for that year is made and litigated years later, when trends in damage awards and inflation could have devalued that amount significantly.

There is one more consideration. The upper limits of coverage available from most carriers reflect to some extent the climate a defendant might find in court at the time those limits are set. Although this does not preclude a judgment coming in for a higher amount than a company normally offers as the upper limit of coverage, it does tend to set a certain informal standard. Predictions about how much might be needed must factor in the possibility that this policy limit may be retroactively applied to a claim to be brought far in the future, when the value of the dollar and the climate of jury awards may have changed appreciably.

How Does PLI Work?

This section will provide you with information on how a typical professional liability policy works. If you have questions about how your policy works under normal or exceptional circumstances, contact your carrier. And keep in mind that the carrier's responsiveness and clarity in addressing your questions may foreshadow how supportive the company would be should a claim arise.

When Does Your Protection Begin?

Most insurance carriers *require* immediate notification of *a threat* of suit as well as of an *actual* suit. It is best to call the carrier immediately for instructions, but it is also wise to follow up that same day with a letter. Thus you guard against any possibility that the carrier may claim you did not comply with their notification provisions and therefore are not eligible for coverage.

However, some psychologists will be surprised to learn that they are protected only against a formal legal complaint. In other words, some policies provide a defense only against "any lawsuit filed against the insured" (or similar language). The carrier is not compelled to provide defense services if the warning signs appear (as opposed to an actual suit being filed) that often precede the filing of a lawsuit. Thus, you may be left to your own devices if you are simply threatened with a suit—a time when your anxiety, confusion, and rage may be at their highest pitch.

Regardless of the status of the suit (threatened or filed), your first impulse might be to contact the client to try to work it out, to argue with the client, to express your anger, or to take other action that could prove counterproductive. However, it may be wisest to find a lawyer, even though your carrier will probably not use that person for your defense once it formally begins to provide a legal defense. Note: Under case law regarding *reservation of rights* letters from carriers, a defendant may be able to have his or her own attorney at the carrier's expense.

Does the Carrier's Lawyer Work for You or the Carrier?

Much confusion, anger, and even anguish can be avoided if you understand the legal framework under which the law, you, and the insurance carrier will work. If you are sued, you are the defendant in the lawsuit. Your insurance policy is a contract with the carrier that both compels and gives the exclusive right to the carrier to defend you. The carrier requires this right, because that same policy/contract also makes the carrier liable for any damages that result from the lawsuit, limited by the exclusions and the coverage limits to which you have agreed as terms of the policy.

The carrier will hire an attorney to defend you, but the attorney will work for the carrier, not for you. Technically, the carrier-selected lawyer is compelled to give you a competent defense and will be vulnerable to a malpractice claim should he or she fail to do so. Practically, if the interests of the defendant–practitioner and the carrier diverge, the lawyer may be inclined to protect the interests of his or her client—the carrier. If this should occur, the attorney would be duty-bound to explain any such conflicts to you and to advise you accordingly.

Such a divergence of interests may arise when a monetary settlement will induce the plaintiff to drop all charges and sign a waiver. Insurance company decisions are sometimes driven by statistics and by the economics involved. They also take into consideration the likelihood of successfully defending a bad case. If a settlement will cost less than a court trial (even a victorious trial) or the potential judgment should you lose, the carrier may recommend that you settle, that is, pay the defendant, even though you may not have been professionally negligent and may have been likely to defeat the lawsuit at trial. When the factual situation looks bad for the practitioner, the carrier will have a definite interest in seeking settlement at a reasonable cost. The problem is that one can never predict the final jury outcome, especially if the plaintiff appears to be a sympathetic figure. Regardless of the circumstances, however, you may wish to pursue the suit for other reasons and may want to go to trial.

Some carriers even anticipate this possibility in the language of the policy. The APAIT-endorsed policy, for example, explicitly limits the carrier's liability to the amount the carrier could have achieved if the attorney, the carrier, and the plaintiff could have agreed on a settlement, that is, to total expenses incurred to date plus the proposed settlement for damages. The practitioner has the right to refuse to settle and to press the case further but does so at his or her own risk and expense for any monies beyond that included in the proposed settlement. In other words, the total of legal expenses and damages awarded may exceed the proposed settlement figure, in which case the psychologist is responsible for these additional costs.

If you are concerned about a possible divergence of interest between you and your carrier, take the matter up forthrightly with the attorney. Put the attorney on notice that you are expecting him or her to provide you personally with a defense. This should serve to sensitize the attorney to any possible conflict of interest. If you decide to pursue the case for your own reasons, but the carrier's attorney feels in conflict, he or she should write you a letter, informing you that he or she cannot serve the interests of both you and the carrier at the same time and suggesting that it may be in your own best interest to get your own lawyer and pursue the matter independently. If the attorney is reluctant to provide such a letter, demand one.

Some programs are more supportive of the insured than others. For example, in the APAIT-endorsed program, any settlement requires the practitioner's written consent. The APAIT office surveys psychologists who have had suits filed against them regarding their satisfaction with the legal services they received. The APAIT will assist the psychologist in working with the lawyer, even by working with the psychologist to convince the carrier to transfer the case to someone else should that be needed.

Some PLI programs, however, divest the insured of many of those rights one would normally expect to accrue to a defendant in a civil lawsuit. These policies compel the defendant to accept the carrier's recommendation about settlement as well as the attorney's decisions on other matters. There may be no internal case-review process, forcing a dissatisfied policyholder to go outside for help, perhaps to the state's insurance commissioner or bar association. And any such plea may be subverted by the terms of the contract (the policy) that was freely undertaken. Read your policy and, if necessary, obtain clarification about what the terms really mean when applied under various circumstances.

Most policies instruct you not only to comply with the policy's directives about giving the carrier notice of any problems but also to perform other duties in the aid of your defense. Boiled down, these tend to give the carrier and its attorney effective control over strategy and over many intermediate decisions, even if the ultimate decision about whether to settle a case is reserved for the defendant. Look closely at any provisions that refer to "action against the company" and "assistance/cooperation of the insured." You should focus on the worst-case scenario in which the carrier might try either to evade defending you or to recover its costs after the lawsuit is over. It may be possible to get information about your carrier's history in this touchy area from their legal department or from the state insurance commissioner.

There is another situation in which you may wish to consider retaining your own legal counsel. If the damages demanded exceed the policy limit, or if a jury award may exceed the policy limit, you will not be protected for any award in excess of this limit. The assigned attorney is not responsible to protect you beyond the policy limits. Under these circumstances, you should retain your own attorney to assure that all steps are taken to protect you against losses in excess of the policy limits.

Some policies include monetary compensation for time lost from your practice. This is generally a per diem for actual court appearances and depositions and may have an upper limit. The APAIT-sponsored policy provides $250 per day up to a maximum of $5,000 for such expenses.

What Does the Insurance Contract Really Say?

Standard language in a contract is often heavily biased in favor of the party providing the contract. There is no way to understand your PLI coverage without mastering the policy document. If it's beyond your ken, you should find someone else to do it for you. We focus next on some of the things to look for.

When Is Your Coverage in Force?

You will receive a written policy that acknowledges your premium payment. Check for specific dates of coverage. Most policies are for 1-year terms. Note your termination date in the unlikely event that your carrier fails to send you a renewal form. If you are renewing, have you made your payment in time? If not, is there a grace period? If there is not, you may have practiced for a time without any coverage. Do not unknowingly risk a claim being filed for that period of time. Your carrier may be willing to negotiate a rider to cover this short period or to issue a new policy retroactive to the previous one.

Each year, you will receive a new policy document, even if there are no changes. These documents could be more valuable than stock certificates because they are the only proof of your specific coverage. Never discard an outdated PLI policy.

What Are the Policy Limits?

Most of these have been mentioned elsewhere. Sometimes you can choose a policy that offers a deductible, money that you will have to pay before the company's financial liability begins. However, most PLI policies do not offer a deductible. If there is a deductible, ask when the deductible applies and whether it applies per claim or once in a policy year.

The simplest policy structure covers you for one claim per year, up to the policy limit you have chosen. As already mentioned, most PLI policies offer aggregate coverage as well. Aggregate coverage usually extends to any number of claims in a policy year, until the sum total of these claims would exceed the aggregate limit. However, be clear about whether there is a limit to the number of claims the aggregate covers in a policy year.

If there are co-insured individuals or other professionals actually named as additional insured, find out whether your liability coverage limit applies only once, to the first claim against everyone insured by your policy, or whether each person is covered separately up to the amount of the policy limit. Verify the same conditions with respect to other employees who may not be named on the policy. Usually clerical and nonprofessional employees are automatically covered, but would a suit against them reduce money available to cover a suit against you in the same year?

Most policies state the way money will be spent in the event of a claim. The usual priorities place legal and defense costs first and the payment of damages second. The crucial point is whether these legal and defense expenses are counted toward the liability limit. For example, in the APAIT-endorsed policy, legal fees and defense costs in this policy do not count against the policy's liability limit. If they do, recognize that legal expenses can be substantial when you decide how much coverage to purchase. In many cases that are settled before trial, the legal and defense costs far exceed the money paid to the plaintiff.

Most policies provide coverage restricted to certain locations. The APAIT-endorsed policy covers lawsuits brought in the United States (and its territories and possessions) and in Canada.

Policy Exclusions: Where Are You Left Unprotected?

In the course of professional life, practitioners may encounter a number of legal problems other than claims of negligence. Knowing the events not covered by your policy is essential, especially before a problem develops. Certain activities and types of disputes might lead to a civil lawsuit (or even to constitutional or criminal charges) that you would have to defend without the carrier's financial and legal protection.

Most policies begin by covering the insured for any wrongful act but then list specific kinds of acts that are excluded. Four of the most significant exclusions are complaints involving criminal acts, sexual charges by a client, problems arising from fee disputes, and any action brought by or against another member of the plan.

Criminal acts. It is illegal to cover criminal acts with insurance coverage. If you are sued for negligence under a criminal statute, your insurance neither pays for your defense nor pays damages. Acts of negligence that fall under criminal statutes vary from state to state. For example, some states have criminal statutes for suits involving failure to report child abuse, cruelty to animals, insurance fraud, or sexual relations with a patient. It is important to be familiar with areas of negligence that are considered to be criminal acts under the laws in your state.

Sexual impropriety. Allegations of sexual impropriety account for the greatest single group of claims experienced in the APAIT-endorsed program. Because any sort of sexual involvement with clients is expressly forbidden by the *Ethical Principles,* you might think it consistent for PLI policies to exclude all such claims.

However, the nature of the problem allows no such easy solution. Clients are able to bring such claims based on no evidence other than their own statements. In many alleged situations, there may be no evidence to corroborate or refute the charge, except the testimony of each party—the "he said, she said" situation. Some clients have filed such claims for retaliatory motives. Others have based their claims of sexual impropriety more on fantasy, delusion, and wish fulfillment than on actual events. And of course, some clients have filed suits against practitioners who have engaged in improper behavior. There is little doubt of the potential harm that can be done to a practitioner by even the allegation of sexual misconduct. There is also little doubt about the serious harm done to a client who has been sexually abused by a therapist.

But the interests of the insured are not necessarily best protected by a policy excluding all sexual claims. If this were so, the wrongly accused and innocent practitioner would be at the mercy of his or her accuser. Professional liability carriers respond to these situations in different ways. For example, the APAIT policy provides for the complete defense of a policyholder but will not pay any settlement or damage award greater than $25,000. This cap has a deterrent effect on potential defendants who realize that they will bear the burden for any large damage awards. Other carriers may exclude any claim that has a sexual element, even to the point of refusing to defend the policyholder. Some policies may even fully cover the insured, but the current trend is to limit or deny coverage altogether.

Fee disputes.   Complaints arising from fee disputes are another major cause of litigation. Most problems arise when a practitioner allows a client's bill to run up and then delegates bill collection to an outside agency. When a practitioner sues for payment of bills, a client may countersue for negligence or may file other complaints whose real roots are planted in the issue of the bill.

Action by another plan member.   Many carriers expressly exclude any action against another member of the same insurance plan. They thus avoid a no-win situation, and in the process discourage plan members from escalating personal and professional squabbles to the courts. Another effect of this policy is to reduce the incentive for multiple defendants to try to dodge personal responsibility for a problem by locating the blame on a colleague. No PLI policy provides money to sue someone else.

Other exclusions.   There are often other exclusions that need to be acknowledged. Most PLI policies cover you when you are accused of negligence in the practice of psychology, narrowly defined, and practitioners need to consider whether their counsel to a client is directed exclusively to issues of mental health. The practitioner's motives may be impeccable, but the results of the advice, if shown to cause demonstrable harm, could make the therapist vulnerable for rendering professional counsel beyond his or her competency. Practitioners have been successfully sued for stepping over the line in advising a client about how to handle his or her financial affairs. You are not protected for the legal or financial advice you may give your clients, however integral to your psychological mission such counseling might be. Indeed, for most civil actions that do not flow directly from negligence in fulfilling your duty of care as a psychologist, you are not covered. Included in this list would be any acts that are restricted by law to other categories of professionals, such as the practice of medicine.

Charges Before a Licensing Board or Ethics Committee

Most PLI policies are designed to protect you from civil suits by clients and their representatives. When practitioners must face a licensing board examination or an ethics committee hearing, they are usually not provided with legal services by their carrier. Nor would they be compensated for any financial loss they might incur as a result of the outcome.

One possible mitigating situation involves a hearing triggered by the same events on which a civil suit is based. On occasion, a carrier will also want the attorney they have hired to defend you in the civil suit to aid in your defense at the psychology hearing. Their motive is to guard against what the law terms an *admission against interest* in which you say something in one setting that would be detrimental to your hearing in the other setting. As a result, the attorney will try to preserve all of the rights, evidentiary protections, and the presumption of innocence that you are entitled to at the civil trial, should one commence.

A Practitioner's Actions as a Participant in an Official Body

What about those practitioners who sit on the other side of the table, serving the profession on licensing review boards and ethics committees? Such bodies could not operate with the force of sanction and censure that they have if their members were not protected. This is a prominent issue in the operation of the board or committee, and most often protective Directors and Officers Liability Insurance will have been negotiated between the sponsoring organization and an insurance carrier. The APAIT policy, for example, covers professional services as a member of a formal accreditation or professional review board of hospitals, professional societies, or professional licensing boards.

Why Do You Need Premises Insurance?

Premises insurance protects the insured against accidents and injuries that may happen to individuals who move in and out of the insured's office. Practitioners need such coverage because there are times when suits that are filed for one cause include secondary charges, such as a claim that the plaintiff suffered physical injury on the property of the practitioner. There have also been instances when a client fell or was attacked by another client or was injured in the building in which the practitioner leased space and later sued the practitioner for compensation. Because some PLI policies do not automatically include premises insurance, practitioners should make sure that they have or that they obtain this basic kind of business coverage.

There are times when you might think that your landlord's insurance should cover an accident (for example, one of your clients might fall on the stairs at the front of the building) and that you are certainly not liable. Even if your landlord has a comprehensive liability policy for all accidents that happen on his or her property, you should still consider carrying premises liability insurance. The landlord's policy almost certainly does not compel the landlord's carrier to defend you personally unless you are actually listed on the policy as an additional insured.

As already discussed, the shotgun approach taken by many litigants is a feature of American law. Often when multiple parties are sued over an incident, those who can easily prove that they are not legally responsible will move for a summary dismissal. If granted, the court order will then remove them from the complaint. But even this abbreviated procedure involves legal savvy, and you would be well advised to have an attorney make your case. If you are insured, the responsibility for and cost of this brief defense will be your carrier's. And even should you succeed there, the landlord's carrier may later sue you for negligence and try to recover the cost incurred in the lawsuit.

Moreover, the assumption that you could displace responsibility for something that happens in your office space is shaky. It is more likely that the landlord's policy *does not* cover space that is leased. And even though most accidents to you or your employees will fall within a different system—worker's compensation or private disability insurance—you do not want an ingenious lawyer trying to take advantage of your exposure.

Therefore, premises liability seems necessary. The good news is that your PLI carrier probably offers it. The policy endorsed by the APAIT includes it automatically, unless precluded by state insurance law. Be sure that you understand the limits of coverage. On most policies, damage to contents (such as by fire or flood) or theft is an exclusion, so you may need a rider or a separate policy to cover the physical assets in your office. How much should you purchase? You can estimate your replacement value for contents and property and buy accordingly. As to liability for lawsuits claiming injury, again the cost of $1 million in coverage is probably a bargain. Coverage under the APAIT-endorsed policy extends the full coverage value of the policy to premises liability.

Will Your Insurance Company Always Be Able To Pay?

It is vital for you to know whether a potential carrier or your present carrier is solvent. Professional liability insurance is a volatile business. Most practitioners are not anxious to shop each year for coverage, and all tend to assume that their insurance company is sufficiently solvent to live up to its contractual commitments. *Do not make such assumptions.*

All insurance companies are regulated by state government. Inquire from your state's insurance commissioner whether the company's policyholders are protected by a state-backed guaranty, in the event of carrier bankruptcy. If not, see if they can provide you with information about that company's history, stability, and reliability. All domestic PLI carriers are rated for financial stability by the A. M. Best Company, which publishes a rating guide. Most public libraries have these guides in their reference sections. It is recommended that you purchase insurance only from carriers rated as *A +* or *A*. Insurance carriers rated lower, or not rated at all, are questionable.

Many companies have come and gone, and others have retreated to more predictable and profitable forms of underwriting. Ask the administrator for your plan about the carrier's history and commitment both to the particular plan that you have and to the field of PLI. Some plans incorporate provisions to protect policyholders in the event a carrier discontinues coverage. For example, APAIT's endorsed carrier has been providing quality insurance coverage to APA members since 1976, almost a geological era when it comes to PLI. However, the APAIT has secured a provision from its carrier guaranteeing a 2-year notice before cancellation of coverage in order to provide time to make an easy transition to another carrier. Also, those practitioners who secure occurrence-based coverage are protected for the term for which they paid. However, if a claims-made company suddenly stops offering PLI coverage, then its policyholders must not only find a new carrier but also look for a tail or a reporting rider to cover claims that might arise based on events in a previous year.

Finding Insurance

Finding a carrier that offers you the coverage you want, and maintaining it over a period of years, may require an industrious search. Shopping for the lowest rate may not be as revealing as comparing the features alternative policies provide. Insurance from a small agency may be available, but the insurance crisis of the 1970s and 1980s has reduced the number of available policies to only a few, underwritten by a handful of large companies. Some carriers may differentiate among practitioners and vary the premium rate accordingly. Others, such as the APAIT-endorsed carrier, provide a simple premium structure and do not vary the rate according to gender, hours, type of practice, or region. The key is to know your needs thoroughly and to make sure that you understand the policies in terms of those needs.

Appendix: The Client's Rights

Listed below are some of the rights generally agreed upon to belong to clients seeking and engaging in therapy. Consumer rights may differ from state to state.

Clients have the right to:

- have full and complete knowledge of the therapist's qualifications and training

- be informed fully regarding the terms under which service will be provided

- discuss their therapy with anyone they choose, including another therapist

- have a detailed explanation of any procedure (whether psychological or medical) or form of therapy that the therapist or any other professional recommends prior to treatment

- refuse evaluation or treatment of any kind unless the right of refusal is limited by law (as in instances of court-ordered evaluation or commitment)

- request summaries of or, in many states, direct access to their files or to have pertinent information in their files shared with another therapist, an organization, or any other party, assuming that the clients provide signed consent if requested to do so

- question the therapist's competence and, if they so desire, to complain to the therapist's superior or to file formal complaints with pertinent professional bodies or legal bodies

- request a copy of ethics codes and other guidelines and procedures that govern the therapist's practice

- terminate therapy at any time or, in the case of court-ordered treatment, refuse to participate in therapy (recognizing that the client may have to face legal consequences as a result of his or her refusal).

References

American Educational Research Association, American Psychological Association, & National Council on Measurement in Education. (1985). *Standards for educational and psychological testing*. Washington, DC: American Psychological Association.

American Psychological Association. (1987). *Casebook on ethical principles of psychologists*. Washington, DC: Author.

American Psychological Association. (1990). Ethical principles of psychologists (amended June 2, 1989). *American Psychologist, 45*, 390–395.

APA Board of Professional Affairs/Committee on Professional Standards. (1981). Specialty guidelines for the delivery of services. *American Psychologist, 36*(6), 639–686.

APA Board of Professional Affairs/Committee on Professional Standards. (1987). General guidelines for providers of psychological services. *American Psychologist, 42*(7), 712–723.

APA Board of Professional Affairs/Committee on Professional Standards, & APA Committee on Psychological Tests and Assessments. (1986). *Guidelines for computer-based tests and interpretations*. Washington, DC: American Psychological Association.

APA Board of Professional Affairs/Task Force on Marketing and Promotion of Psychological Services. (1986). *Marketing psychological services: A practitioner's guide*. Washington, DC: American Psychological Association.

APA Committee on Academic Freedom and Conditions of Employment. (1987). Guidelines for conditions of employment of psychologists. *American Psychologist, 42*(7), 724–729.

APA Ethics Committee. (1985). Rules and procedures. *American Psychologist, 40*(6), 685–694.

Schutz, B. M. (1982). *Legal liability in psychotherapy: A practitioner's guide to risk management*. San Francisco: Jossey-Bass.

VandenBos, G. R., & Duthie, R. F., (1986). Confronting and supporting colleagues in distress. In R. R. Kilburg, P. E. Nathan, & R. W. Thoreson (Eds.), *Professionals in distress: Issues, syndromes, and solutions in psychology* (pp. 211–231). Washington, DC: American Psychological Association.

Bibliography

The list that follows is by no means a definitive list of publications related to mental health ethics, practice standards, law, and liability. The fact that they appear here does not imply endorsement. Rather, the items listed are particularly useful in that, as individual publications, they provide a significant body of information in one place that might otherwise be found only if you examine numerous sources, or because they provide interesting viewpoints on a particular issue. Many of the publications have excellent and lengthy references lists.

American Psychological Association. (1987, August, amended). *Bylaws of the American Psychological Association*. Washington, DC: Author. (Available from APA Governance Services, 1200 Seventeenth St., N.W., Washington, DC 20036.)

American Psychological Association Insurance Trust. (n.d.). *What is insurance?* Washington, DC: Author.

APA Board of Professional Affairs/Committee on Professional Practice. (1985). *A hospital practice primer for psychologists*. Washington, DC: American Psychological Association.

APA Board of Professional Affairs/Committee on Professional Practice. (1987). Model act for state licensure of psychologists. *American Psychologist, 42*(7), 696–703.

APA Board of Professional Affairs/Committee on Professional Practice and Committee on Professional Standards. (1981, Fall). *Psychologists' use of physical interventions*. Report of the Task Force on Psychologists' Use of Physical Intervention. Washington, DC: American Psychological Association.

APA Board of Professional Affairs/Committee on Professional Standards. (1988). Casebook for providers of psychological services. *American Psychologist, 43*(7), 557–563. (This update appears periodically in *American Psychologist* and contains new case examples prepared by the Board of Professional Affairs/Committee on Professional Standards.)

Applebaum, P. S., & Roth, L. H. (1984). Involuntary treatment in medicine and psychiatry. *American Journal of Psychiatry, 141*(2), 202–205.

Beck, J. C. (Ed.) (1985). *The potentially violent patient and the Tarasoff decision in psychiatric practice*. Washington, DC: American Psychiatric Press.

Beis, E. B. (1984). *Mental health and the law*. Rockville, MD: Aspen Systems Corporation.

Bernard, J. L., Murphy, M., & Little, M. (1987). The failure of clinical psychologists to apply understood ethical principles. *Professional Psychology: Research and Practice, 18*(5), 489–491.

Blau, T. H. (1984). *The psychologist as expert witness*. New York: John Wiley & Sons.

Bray, J. H., Shepherd, J. N., & Hays, J. R. (1985). Legal and ethical issues in informed consent to psychotherapy. *The American Journal of Family Therapy, 13*(2), 50–60.

Brooks, A. D. (1974). *Law, psychiatry, and the mental health system*. Boston: Little, Brown & Co.

Cohen, R. J. (1979). *Malpractice: A guide for mental health professionals*. New York: The Free Press.

Cohen, R. J., & Mariano, W. E. (1982). *Legal guidebook in mental health*. New York: The Free Press.

Cooke, G. (Ed.) (1980). *The role of the forensic psychologist*. Springfield, IL: Charles C Thomas.

Everstine, L., & Everstine, D. S. (Eds.) (1986). *Psychotherapy and the law*. Orlando: Grune & Stratton.

Ewing, C. P. (Ed.) (1985). *Psychology, psychiatry, and the law: A clinical and forensic handbook*. Sarasota, FL: Professional Resource Exchange, Inc.

Gustafson, K. E., & McNamara, J. R. (1987). Confidentiality with minor clients: Issues and guidelines for therapists. *Professional Psychology: Research and Practice, 18*(5), 503–508.

Gutheil, T. G., & Applebaum, P. S. (1982). *Clinical handbook of psychiatry and the law*. New York: McGraw-Hill.

Haas, L. J., & Malouf, J. L. (1989). *Keeping up the good work: A practitioner's guide to mental health ethics*. Sarasota, FL: Professional Resource Exchange, Inc.

Hare-Mustin, R. T., Marecek, J., Kaplan, A. G., & Liss-Levinson, N. (1979). Rights of clients, responsibilities of therapists. *American Psychologist, 34*(1), 3–16.

Keith-Spiegel, P., & Koocher, G. P. (1985). *Ethics in psychology: Professional standards and cases*. New York: Random House. (Note: This publication is copyrighted by Newbery Award Records and distributed exclusively by Lawrence Erlbaum Associates, Inc., Hillsdale, New Jersey.)

Klein, J. I., Macbeth, J. E., & Onek, J. N. (1984). *Legal issues in the private practice of psychology*. Washington, DC: American Psychiatric Press.

Knapp, S., & VandeCreek, L. (1981). Behavioral medicine: Its malpractice risks for psychologists. *Professional Psychology, 12*(6), 677–683.

Miller, D. J., & Thelen, M. H. (1987, Winter). Confidentiality in psychotherapy: History, issues, and research. *Psychotherapy, 24*(4), 704–711.

Monahan, J. (1981). *Predicting violent behavior: An assessment of clinical techniques*. Beverly Hills, CA: Sage.

Sales, B. D. (Ed.) (1983). *The professional psychologist's handbook*. NY: Plenum Publishing.

Soisson, E. L., VandeCreek, L., & Knapp, S. (1987). Thorough record keeping: A good defense in a litigious era. *Professional Psychology: Research and Practice, 18*(5), 498–502.

Tryon, G. S. (1986). The professional practice of psychology. Edited by G. R. Caddy. Norwood, NJ: Ablex Publishing Corporation.

VandeCreek, L., Knapp, S., & Herzog, C. (1987, Summer). Malpractice risks in the treatment of dangerous patients. *Psychotherapy, 24*(2), 145–153.

Woody, R. H. (1988). *Fifty ways to avoid malpractice: A guidebook for mental health professionals*. Sarasota, FL: Professional Resource Exchange, Inc.

Yamamoto, J., Acosta, F. X., Evans, L. A., & Skilbeck, W. M. (1984). Orienting therapists about patients' needs to increase patient satisfaction. *American Journal of Psychiatry, 141*(2), 274–277.